JACKIE'S MIRACLE

Emeka Iwenofu

I0108238

HOPE POINT PRESS

CLEVELAND

Hope Point Press
PO Box 110452
Cleveland, OH 44111

Cover design by Nate Myers of Wilhelm Design

Photograph of front cover by Johnny Stephaun Smagola
Photograph of author by Johnny Stephaun Smagola

Editor: Connie Garofoli

Library of Congress Cataloging-in-Publication Data;

ISBN: 978-0-9855321-2-3
LCCN: 2012909468

jackiesmiracle.com
Iwenofu, Emeka, Author
Jackie's Miracle / Emeka Iwenofu.

ePDF ISBN: 978-0-9855321-0-9
ePUB ISBN: 978-0-9855321-1-6

1. Self-Help 2. Inspirational Book 3. Spirituality I. Iwenofu, Emeka, Author—Early Release

10 9 8 7 6 5 4 3 2 1

All Praises to Jackie's Miracle

"*This book is a lovely and easy way for people to open up to the Law of Attraction. It's particularly sweet in that it takes the reader through someone's tough life journey; how they are taught and then utilize LOA to change everything in their life. I think this book (and the Miracle Trilogy series) should be available in prisons, libraries, schools and for all children and teenagers, so they have these tools. It's an easy and inspiring read. Highly recommended!*"

—Deborah Dachinger

Host of Emmy Award Winning Show: *Dare to Dream Radio*
Best Selling author of *Wisdom to Success: The Surefire Secrets to Accomplish All Your Dreams*

"*The very meeting of Emeka was purely the Law of Attraction at its best. It's no surprise the story he tells in* Jackie's Miracle *is the practical application of how the Law of Attraction can actually be taught and applied to anyone who desires more out of life. I was so captivated by the realness of the characters that I forgot about the science and gained a true understanding inside the story. Be prepared to be touched, moved and inspired!*"

—Valerie Waugaman, Co-Founder of FITmission.com
"*SIREN*" on NBC's *American Gladiators*
Youth Empowerment Leader

This is for the men and women who've given up all hope in life for whatever reason.

May this book be the solution, inspiration and guide to all that you seek in life.

Live abundantly and be happy.

You are STILL an awesome wonder!

People are always blaming their circumstances for what they are. I don't believe in circumstances. The people who get on in this world, are the people who get up and look for the circumstances they want, and if they can't find them, make them.

—George Bernard Shaw

Contents

Preface

IF I WERE TO THINK BACK TO WHEN I FIRST FELL IN LOVE
with the pen, it would have to be when I was 12 years old
and given a writing assignment by my seventh grade teacher,
Mrs. Benson, who later said that she enjoyed my story. But
if I were to look back to what rooted my talent, I would have
to go back to the summer between my fourth and fifth-grade
school years with my dad. In order for me to make myself
"useful" throughout the summer, rather than watching TV
all the time, he'd drop me off with a snack bag at the library
before he went to work at 8 a.m. and told me to stay there
until he returned from work at 4:30. So in essence, I would
be at the library for nearly 8 hours as a means to make myself
useful, which for me was to read.

Well, I was not into reading at first. In fact, I hated it,
which was why I looked forward to the summer. But with
what my father was suddenly implementing for the summer,
made me hate it immensely. In fact, I felt my father was being

way too harsh on me; almost like he hated me, that I became anxious in knowing if there was some help line service out there that I could report to since I thought this whole act was illegal and a form of child abuse.

Within the first couple days at the library, I grew frustrated and restless, and began annoying the librarians, since I could never stay still at one place. But since it was clear that this was going to be my summer, I eventually picked up "something" to make the best of it. I first started with comic books before actually finding books that seemed interesting. Within a short time, I began bringing books home, suddenly enjoying them, from which my imagination began to take a life of its own, which compelled me to write little short stories by myself, which I enjoyed a lot. As time went on past the seventh grade, I began to get very serious about writing, to where I attended free writers' workshops and wrote two novels on my own by the age of 15 which didn't go anywhere, but convinced me enough that writing was my calling and that I could become a great writer if I was really serious.

As time passed, I decided on getting a major in literature and English from college, which my father later objected to, claiming that I would starve to death. So, as a result, in order to make both my parents "happy", I enrolled at Cleveland State University and took on a much more "sensible" major, which was accounting, since I had somewhat of a gift with crunching numbers in my head. For a while, everything went well and I was due to graduate in a few months, until my life took a whole different direction, one that would alter my path forever.

I was suddenly fired from a federal government position and later with the city government. At that point, I began working a number of odd jobs that were short lived since I had trouble keeping the previous one. At the same time, I was struggling in business ventures of my own, hoping to become a successful entrepreneur based on what was continuing to happen to me in the job market. It was during this time that I began to engage and observe the street life and victims of broken homes, abuse, crime and dysfunctional families. I took mental notes of what I was seeing, learning about their stories, which were totally different from the world I came from that was for the most part, a stable and "normal" setting.

At this time, I began to hate my situation by not being able to provide for myself and having to endure all these massive setbacks without any reasonable breakthrough in sight, and no real explanation of why this was happening. From that point on, I was literally depressed, in despair, and very negative, blaming the system, government, and other institutions for my problems since this was a route I had never anticipated I would ever be in since leaving college. During this time, in order to survive, I became an avid shoplifter (which I felt I was very good at by the way). I also went to abandoned houses, took aluminum and copper, and sold them as scrap metal, while also selling unlawful items to survive. I spent a brief time in corrections for my acts, where I felt I was nothing more than a bitter disappointment to myself and my family; a man wandering about aimlessly without any clear answers or direction in life.

I must say however that it was a pure blessing that I never resorted to alcohol or any other self destructive behavior during this crisis, because I was literally lost.

But as fate would have it, on the day of my birthday, I got a letter in the mail offering me to listen to a CD set on how to obtain success in my life and live the life I always wanted. The cost of the set was $300. At that moment, all I had was $75 along with my car that had no engine in it, which I was going to scrap anyway to get the $300. It was all the money I had to my name that I was now going to use to pay for the course, on strict faith, since I was desperate for a miracle and prayed that this would be the solution to all my problems.

The set ended up becoming the most important investment I had ever made in my life. My whole outlook on life changed, and as a result I read over 20 different books on success and positive principles instructed by the set, which eventually engineered the idea of me writing my first novel as an adult called *Jackie's Miracle*, to share to the world the lessons on how anyone can achieve success throughout all bitter circumstances. This was the start of The Miracle Trilogy® series that I published through my company, Hope Point Press.

Francine's Miracle is the first part of the series. The story is of a young Irish immigrant named Francine who immigrates to America during the 1920s. Her family consists of a drunk father, a bitter mother, tragedy, poverty and verbal abuse. She desperately seeks an escape from her problems, so as to enter a better life. It is when she meets a stranger through a twist of fate--who educates her on how to achieve her dreams which forms as a blue print for any reader to do the same in their own lives. It is after Francine applies these techniques and gets her "miracle" that she eventually becomes a mentor in the second book, *Mandi's Miracle*, which takes place during the civil rights movement in 1960s Mississippi.

Mandi is cancer-ridden at a very young age, and receives her "miracle" from mentor Francine, before becoming a parole officer and mentor to ex-con, Jackie. *Jackie's Miracle* takes place in the present day, and tells the story of a young woman who lifts herself up from a life of the streets, abuse, drugs, crime, and addiction to personal prosperity and happiness.

I have received tremendous praises by numerous readers throughout the world from reading these books already, through my internet blogs or just on the street and hope that they will continue to have a massive and everlasting impact on many more people to come. In just under two years, *Jackie's Miracle* has been translated into Japanese with *Francine's*

Miracle next on the way. And because of its impact, I know that there's more translations expected in the near future; all because I just made the decision to write!

But if I were to look back on my life, as to what led me to this point, I would say that everything I have experienced was well worth the price, in order to share the idea and knowledge that hope and change are attainable which is why I am so gracious of my past and wouldn't change a thing, since I now know that it was all part of the journey that led me to what I was meant to do in the first place, which is write, and most importantly, share these lessons that can help change a society and impact a culture that so desperately needs it, since that now has become my personal mission and passion in life.

In all, God bless you all, enjoy, and I hope this book helps you realize what's possible, in order to help you achieve your goals and dreams!

—Emeka Iwenofu

PS: Thank you dad for helping me find my talent. You truly knew what you were doing all along and I love you!

1

❧❧❧

Early Release

JAQUITA SAT IN THE TOP BUNK OF HER 8 BY 5-FOOT CELL, waiting for the early morning to arrive. However, since there were no windows, it would only be the sudden bright lights from the ceiling that would signal the time, followed by a loud shout given by a guard, commanding everyone to wake up. Normally, JaQuita would have been sleeping by now. But this time, it was different. She had not slept a wink that night, even though the lights had been out since 10 p.m. and the building was practically silent. The only noise she heard was the loud snoring of her cell mate in the bottom bunk, Shamika Jackson, or in her case, M1400950. That was her prison number. Though, when one shares the same cell with the same person for 18 months, they can get used to such noises.

As she waited, JaQuita began thinking about her past and all the events that led her to this point. She was a young woman, age 23, with a complexion of hot chocolate—not too light and not too dark. However, her youthful appearance was often overshadowed by the mood in her eyes. Anyone who stared at her face could easily see the layers of sorrow, pain and despair within. The slight roughness of her cheeks and forehead showed signs of a woman with a troubled past—someone who hadn't been fortunate in the life that had been offered thus far.

Her mother, Brenda Jenkins, died when she was 13. And there was no point of even mentioning her father because she never knew him, due to her mother's random affairs with men, JaQuita figured. After her mother's death, JaQuita had moved from different foster homes, feeling slightly loved by different families. However, nothing could erase the scars and painful memories she had endured as a child. The neglect, verbal and sexual abuse still haunted her to this day. Anytime she would think back, she would either break down crying, or get mad at the world, feeling she was worthless.

Yet, prison was no place to find anyone who cared about anyone else. Everyone had a story. The majority of the prisoners came from broken homes, abusive childhoods, violence, criminal families—or other prisons. So, JaQuita's case was no different. Besides, there was always someone else who had a more painful past to share. The bottom line was, in prison, one had to be strong. The motto was, "Do your time. Don't let your time do you." And besides, where else was a prisoner going to go? The only hope for an ex-con was that once she leaves, she doesn't become violent or mentally insane when out on the streets. Hopefully, from all that the person had been through, there would be something she could learn from to change her life around. Yet if the prison mentality was too strongly ingrained in her, it was only a matter of time before she would be right back to jail.

After several hours, the lights finally appeared, thus signaling for everyone to arise.

"Rise 'n shine, ladies! Get up! Get up!" screamed a female guard.

Immediately, all the ladies got up. One guard began walking down the hallway, peaking into every cell on her left. During the process, she held a baton, which rubbed against each cell gate as she moved past, thus alerting the inmates to take notice, as if they had not already. It was a loud—and annoying—sound. Three other guards were doing the same; each on their own respective floors.

The name of the prison was called *Valerie State Correctional Facility*. It was composed of many acres of land. Inside were four floors of jail cells, two separate floors on both sides of the prison. Each floor contained 34 cell blocks, with each cell holding two inmates. Therefore, there were 68 prisoners on each floor. When you multiply that by four floors, you get 272 total prisoners. To even get to that area from the outside, one had to go through five security doors, where the walkways were patterned like a maze. It was a female prison. The women there were convicted of both violent and non-violent crimes—assault, armed robbery, kidnapping, burglary, drug trafficking, fraud, theft and murder. There was a list of other offences, but those were the most common. A few of the women were innocent, but most were not.

The prison was based in Waushaw, Michigan, which was a farm town with a small population, located near the southern border of the state. Residents of the town were either farmers or small business owners. The residential and business areas, however, were far from the prison, which was deep in a forest, away from anyone traveling along the roadway. No one could make a mistake and just stumble upon the facility. The prison itself was about three miles from the main road. That way, there were no distractions.

It had the usual high tower, where at least one guard with an assault rifle stood at the top, overseeing the entire premises all hours of the day. There was a basketball court, weight sets, a few benches and a large area of green grass that stretched along the perimeter. A concrete area sat in the center of the property. Surrounding the entire premises were 8-foot-tall barbed wire fences with 10 surveillance cameras aimed at almost every angle outside of the building. Therefore, it was pretty apparent that no one who had even the slightest grain of sanity would ever try to escape, unless of course, they were already suicidal or on death row.

It had been JaQuita's home for 4 years, 3 months and 5 days. She was convicted of aggravated assault and armed robbery. When she was free, she and a friend named Jodi robbed a corner store to get money to buy pharmaceuticals. In the process, the store manager, who was being robbed at gun point by Jodi, stalled enough so that the police were notified by outsiders who were witnessing the whole act through a large glass window. As the police entered, Jodi immediately turned and opened fire. One of the officers ducked while the other rolled down to the nearest corner and shot Jodi, who instantly fell to the floor from a bullet to the abdomen. She laid there bleeding.

JaQuita, not knowing what to do, ran in the opposite direction, heading for the back door. The two officers began chasing her. As they ran, JaQuita pushed one of the store racks down to block them. But as she opened the back door, she was captured by another officer, who had been waiting in the alley. JaQuita managed to break loose for a moment, but the officer remained persistent and grabbed her by the arm. JaQuita then turned around swiftly and began punching the officer mercilessly in the face and stomach, kicking him a few times. Shocked by her strength, the officer fell to the ground, but somehow managed to hold onto one of her feet, restraining her temporarily until the other two officers arrived. Finally, the three of them managed to subdue her and eventually arrest her. They found a knife in her pocket.

Out of revenge, the badly injured officer struck JaQuita hard in the face. She was defenseless, as a result of her hands being tied behind her back. She was eventually picked up by another officer who threw her in the back of the police cruiser. She suffered a gash to the left cheek just an inch below her eye. It was her first offense.

JaQuita was recalling all of this while waiting for the machine to open her cell door. At that instant, she thought of Jodi, who was pronounced dead the day after the incident. Sometimes, JaQuita would ask herself why she wasn't the one shot. To her, she saw nothing left to enjoy in this world. The world had been such a cold and miserable place for her for so long. All she really had that kept her going throughout her years in prison was her diary, which she kept close to her side. It contained all of the things she had been through in her life.

The cell doors on each floor opened, and a straight line was formed by all the inmates outside the cell doors. No one was to move just yet. Within a few minutes, each guard began rattling off each inmate's number. When the prisoner heard her number, she was to just yell "present." At Valerie State, as with most prisons, the prisoners weren't called by name. They were called by their prison number. That was their name. And it was their job to remember it at all times.

JaQuita's number was M6700015. As soon as the guard called it, she yelled "present." After that was completed, the guards ordered the inmates to remain in a single line. They were going to the auditorium, where they would collect their empty trays to receive the breakfast that awaited them. What they got was stale cereal, milk, a banana and a small scoop of applesauce.

As soon as JaQuita collected her meal, she went over to a round table where three of her friends were sitting. When she got there, she sat down and started to eat. She had only five minutes to finish, which was the rule of the prison.

"So how does it feel to know you fine'ly gettin' out this bitch?" asked Stacy, who was beside her.

JaQuita thought for a moment, then shrugged her shoulders. "Mmm… I own know. I guess I'm a find out," she answered. "You got family waitin' on ya?" asked another woman, named Latisha.

"Naw. I mean ain't nobody got time for me. Everyone's… *dead.*"

"But you ain't comin' back, is you?" Stacy asked.

JaQuita then thought about it. "You know, I'own know," she said laughing. Soon after, everyone at the table began laughing. All of a sudden, another inmate who heard the conversation from another table, began shouting, "she'll be back."

Though JaQuita paid her no attention. She then added. "But I ain't no punk. I'm a hustle and get it however I can. You feel me? Ain't nothin' go'n stop me from makin' sumthin'… 'cause now, I got ta survive."

"I hear that," replied Latisha.

At that instant, a bell rang signaling that breakfast was over. The inmates had to get up and when their table was called, empty their trays before placing them in a tall stack on top of the counter. After completing this task, they were to go back to their table and wait for any special announcements of the day or special letters to be received. If there were none, they were notified of that too. Though today, JaQuita was definitely going to hear some special news. She, along with six other ladies, came up to a guard, who then told them in private to prepare their things in the next two hours so that they could vacate the prison. A bus was going to be arriving at 11 a.m. that would take them back to Detroit, where they would go through a few formalities before finally being released to the free world.

JaQuita was now a bit excited, because to finally hear that she was leaving for good meant that it was official. It was really true. She was really leaving. After four years, she was going to be gone. The judge originally sentenced her to 5-7 years in prison, however after close scrutiny of her behavior while there, the State eventually decided that it was safe to release her early under *watch* provisions. JaQuita was a woman who kept mostly to herself and rarely caused any problems for other people. She respected authority and did as she was told for the most part.

As she packed her things with her diary in her pocket, she began thinking of her four years behind bars. There weren't many happy moments to remember of the place. However, there were some people with whom she grew a close bond. Those women she would miss. And before she stood in line by the door with the other six inmates scheduled to be released that day, she went to hug her closest friends; some cried, but all knew it was for the better. Some of them offered words of encouragement for her not to come back, while others just waved goodbye. After about an hour of waiting, another guard finally appeared, ready to escort them out. As soon as this happened, all seven women heard loud cheers of chanting and raving filling the air. They then turned back one last time, waving and smiling to everyone before they faded from their presence, away from them for good.

As for the prison, it always stayed full. Another batch of women were coming the following morning to fill those empty cells.

The drive back to Detroit would take a total of three hours, including breaks and gas fill-ups. Once they arrived, they would be sent to the main police department, where the staff would release their personal belongings, cut off their ID bracelets, allow them to remove their prison uniforms and fill out any paperwork. Since none of the seven women had completed their full sentences, they each were given a packet that contained the name of their assigned parole officer they were to see, which was mandatory. Once that was received, the ladies, now ex-convicts, were free to go.

Some of the women had families waiting to pick them up. The others would have to look for a temporary home or a shelter until they could get back on their feet. In JaQuita's case, she was going to be on parole for at least a year. Under that condition, she was to report to the parole office within a week of her release. Failure to comply with the State's conditions would result in a violation that could possibly send her back to prison. While on parole, she could not get into any other trouble with the law, and had to take random urine tests to make sure she was not using narcotics.

As the bus loaded up, ready to take off, all JaQuita could do was sit next to a window and day dream. As the bus drove off, she thought of her mother, Brenda Jenkins.

Brenda was a woman who grew up in the '50s. From the moment she was born, it was apparent that she was doomed from the start. Her father, who was an alcoholic, left her when she was 7. Before he left, she witnessed him physically abusing her mother on numerous occasions. Her mother, on the other hand, was no better. She was known for cheating on Brenda's father, which often resulted in such punishment. When he left, her mother invited different men to the house and would lie to Brenda, claiming they were all her uncles. Brenda, at the time, was too young to think otherwise, but saw a lot unfold before her innocent eyes. She could smell the alcohol that was always on the breaths of her "uncles" when they walked in. Almost everyday, she watched them gather in the smoky living room. When she was 12, she was molested for the first time by her mother's live-in boyfriend. When she told her mother about it, her mother slapped her to the floor, claiming that she just didn't like the man. When it became apparent that Brenda *wasn't* lying, her mother allowed the man to continue to live with them, placing the man before her own daughter.

Heartbroken by all this, Brenda ran away to stay with her father in Flint, Michigan. Though it wasn't any better. Her father continued to drink heavily and would slap his girlfriends repeatedly in front of Brenda. Along with this came the harsh words Brenda would receive from her father, always in a loud fashion. Brenda still felt safe, because at least she knew the sexual abuse had stopped. Yet the constant physical abuse, which she witnessed more times than she could count, convinced her that beating a woman was common in any relationship, and that any man who didn't hit a woman didn't love her.

At the age of 16, Brenda started to hang out with high school friends who lured her into prostitution. Now at this time, all of them were already prostituting. The four of them stayed in one house, where each woman had their own bedroom. The owner of the place was a pimp known as "*Slik,*" who thought of himself more as a manager or "*female assistant.*" However, all the girls called him "Daddy." Slik was a 45-year-old black man with a large afro, who was very powerful at persuading a woman to follow his orders. He wore sharp suits with big sunglasses, often driving around in a Cadillac looking for women who were vulnerable and had nothing. He promised them that they would make thousands working for him. He promised them a house where they'd have no expenses. According to him, all they had to do was work for him three times a week soliciting men on the corner or track, as it was called.

While with him, the girls learned how to manipulate men, steal from them, and engage in all kinds of other activity that would get Slik his money. Slik did take the girls shopping from time to time, but the work that was involved in supporting him was tremendous. Slik told them that they would only work part time, but they worked every day for almost about 12 hours. And heaven forbid if Slik wasn't paid after a few hours' work. There was hell to pay. The slap that

Slik would inflict on his girls was sometimes enough to shatter bone. His hand was that strong.

To make matters worse, he got them addicted to cocaine. Cocaine was the main ingredient he used to control all his women. With cocaine, they were powerless, unable to use their minds to think rationally or discover logical solutions to their problems. As long as he was supplying the dope every once in a while, they went nowhere. It didn't matter how many times he beat them, they all came back, since in their twisted minds, he loved them, as their dope man. Therefore, they were trapped. Psychologically, they were powerless. By controlling their minds he controlled them.

Brenda, who was involved fully with the lifestyle, endured every abuse imaginable. Unfortunately for Slik, cocaine had a way of backfiring. Depending on how addicted the girls were, they would occasionally break the rules, trading sex for drugs instead of money. Besides Slik, there were several other drug dealers that the girls knew, and who they eventually slept with in exchange for heroin or cocaine. Sometimes, the money the girls received went to the drug dealers instead of Slik's pocket.

Brenda, who did this often, was beaten repeatedly by Slik, which often resulted in a bloody nose and/or a black eye. After a while, she could no longer work until the bruises healed. But one night, rather than wait, Brenda went out when no one was home and stole all of Slik's jewelry (and everything else of value) and escaped to Detroit to live with her twin sister, Maggie. Little did Brenda know, Slik was gunned down two weeks later over a dispute with another pimp, who claimed that Slik stole one of his girls. That act, whether true or not, was considered disrespectful to another pimp's livelihood and the "game" as well. In the end it would appear that Slik wasn't so "slick" after all.

However, it was in Detroit where Brenda got out of control. Brenda knew the prostitution business well enough that she decided to continue working, but this time on her own. She didn't need a pimp, as far she was concerned. At this stage, prostitution was all she knew and was what she was really good at. The problem was that rather than respecting the rules of the game, she continued partaking in sex for free, sharing herself mostly with men who didn't even use condoms. There was no telling what kind of diseases they brought with them. Still, Brenda didn't care and within four months of leaving Flint, became pregnant at age 19.

Obviously, Brenda wasn't ready for a child. She saw it as another responsibility and distraction from all the fun she felt she was having. Many times she contemplated aborting the baby. However, she was more fearful of the abortion procedure than of having a child. So she felt it just wasn't worth it. Besides, she never could save enough money to afford the abortion anyway.

So, in the summer of the following year, Brenda gave birth to a baby girl and named her JaQuita. Since the name was unique, Brenda reasoned, that same uniqueness would somehow appear in the baby's character, in a good sense, once she developed. Brenda came from a family of abuse and violence, and she hoped that in some divine way, such a name might change the cycle. That was her only prayer.

But sadly, motherhood did little to change Brenda. Often times, the baby was left unattended while Brenda did whatever she could to make herself feel better. Sometimes Maggie was left with caring for baby. It soon got to a point when Maggie threatened to go to the courts to gain full custody of JaQuita, though she hesitated, fearing that the court might end up sending the baby to a foster home, since Maggie had no clean record either.

As JaQuita grew up, she began observing abusive behavior similar to what her mother saw when she was a child. Brenda also became very skinny. On the streets, she was notorious as a whore and drug addict. JaQuita learned this, when at the age of 11, she was dressed up by her mother and forced to offer her body to a drug dealer so that her mother could feed her drug habit. It was a horrific experience, and nearly made JaQuita collapse once it was over. This occurred a few more times up until age 13.

One might think that Brenda, by this time, would have some sense of motherhood, and that certain things would be off limits. However, that wasn't the case. She was so addicted to drugs that nothing mattered to her anymore. Men would have their way with her and she didn't care. She didn't care about anyone much less herself. And one could easily predict that it would only be a matter of time before she would eventually meet her demise.

So, early one morning, JaQuita woke up to get something to eat. She checked in the fridge, but nothing was there. Brenda had told her that she would buy groceries the evening before, but that never happened. So out of frustration, JaQuita went to complain to her mom about the lack of food, which obviously was far from being the first time. But when JaQuita went to Brenda's room, she noticed her mother laying on the edge of the bed, motionless. Her left arm hung off the bed nearly touching the floor. Wrapped around her left wrist was a belt that nearly came off. For a moment, JaQuita assumed Brenda was getting high or just plain tired. But when she looked closer, she noticed that her mother's eyes, which were still open, hadn't blinked for several minutes. On the floor, near the mattress, was residue of white powder, along with a couple of syringes, a crack pipe and cotton balls. Still, Brenda just lay there, with what appeared to be dried foam coming from her mouth. JaQuita, now a little scared, began tapping her mother.

"Mom?" she questioned. There was no response.

JaQuita then pushed her a little harder, calling her name, again. Still, there was no answer.

"Mom!" she yelled. Again, nothing happened.

Frantic, JaQuita began shaking her mother back and forth with all her might, before breaking down crying.

"MOM!" she screamed. "MOM-MYYYYYYYYYYYY!"

Maggie, who heard all this, came in to see what was going on, only to scream as well, knowing that her sister was dead. Within an hour the police came and took Brenda's lifeless body on a stretcher, covered her face with a white blanket and wheeled her away to the city morgue. The official report later concluded that she died of a heroin overdose. She was 33.

Traumatized and distraught, JaQuita just wanted to die. Her mother, who wasn't much of a mother, was dead. And even though Brenda was a horrible woman, she was still JaQuita's mother, and she was the closest family JaQuita had, despite all her shortcomings. It was a twisted tale that only could be understood by those who experienced it. JaQuita still loved her mother, regardless. If anything, she brought her life. And that alone had to mean something. Maggie appeared to be the next likely candidate for custody of JaQuita, but when her record was pulled up, it was discovered that she had outstanding warrants for not appearing in court for felony charges, and was thus hauled off to prison. JaQuita had no known family members who would take her now. She knew very little about her grandparents since her mother rarely spoke of them. And it wouldn't have mattered anyway. By this time Brenda's father had died and her mother was in a mental hospital, always twitching her feet uncontrollably.

As a result, the State had no other option but to place JaQuita Jenkins, or JJ as many would call her, in a foster home. So at age 14, JaQuita was sent off to live with foster parents. She was enrolled in school and gradually acquired a love for reading and writing. Those activities eventually put her mind at ease. To her, reading was a way to enter a world where reality was at rest. She enjoyed that. Yet socially, she had difficulty making friends and showed a violent temper at times.

By the time she reached 18, she had already been to three foster homes and had dropped out of the tenth grade. Without anyone to guide her, she entered a life of drinking and partying. Marijuana was the drug of choice for her, along with pills that later followed. According to her, those two elements gave her some form of escape from all the pain she had endured. Next, boys became her interest. And with that came sex. JaQuita was never in a serious relationship, however. It was just sex to her, she thought. No loyalty. No strings attached. Just sex. It had to be by some divine miracle that she never became pregnant, since at times, the boys didn't wear protection.

Since she was 18, JaQuita no longer needed to be in a foster home, and therefore stayed with Peanut, whose real name was Patty Pratt Jacobs. Peanut was a white heavyset lady who had been a friend of JaQuita's since the second grade. Her family knew all about JaQuita and welcomed her to stay with them, knowing the trauma she had endured. Peanut survived by selling weed and pills, and encouraged JaQuita to use them to ease her mind. JaQuita would try the pills and liked them, but after a while Peanut stopped offering them because JaQuita wasn't contributing anything financially.

It was then that JaQuita joined Jodi to rob the convenience store, which eventually landed her in prison. And now, here she was, four years later, travelling to Detroit to finally get a second chance on life.

2

❦

Metrohouse

A S SOON AS THE BUS ARRIVED IN DETROIT, IT WENT TO the downtown police station where the former inmates would be briefed on their cases and a few other details before finally being released. JaQuita couldn't wait to enter the station so that she could finally rest her feet and possibly eat something. She was hungry.

The bus entered the station's garage, where the women were escorted out of the vehicle and into the building. They waited inside a room where their papers were being prepared. The wait was long—like an hour and a half long. Yet to these women, they knew nothing else but to wait, since *waiting* was all that they did since their sentencing. Therefore, this was nothing to them.

They were each called to take off their green uniforms and dress in the street clothes they wore when they entered prison. They were given back all of the possessions that they had when they were apprehended. JaQuita had on jean overalls along with a baseball cap, both of which had a strange smell. Her brown boots they gave back to her appeared worn out. In addition to these she was given a few other clothing items that had been delivered to her by Peanut and her family. The guards placed them in a bag, which JaQuita could carry off with her.

Next, the prison wristbands were cut off, which gave the women a tremendous feeling of joy. To actually wear that for years and finally have it removed gave a relief that was almost inexplicable. Once that was done, they each received their letters of release and instructions as to where they were to appear to find out who their parole officer would be. As soon as that was over, they were assigned out of the building. They were now free.

All the women were ecstatic and yelled outside as a few of their family members awaited them with open arms. No one was coming for JaQuita, but she was still happy. So for several minutes, she stood outside the department, then sat down and thought about the past. The fact that she was now free took a while for her to digest. Four years in jail was a long time. Being told everyday what to do and not having the ability to behave how she wanted was a life of virtual slavery, she thought. So for her to retrain her mind and start living a life of freedom was something that was going to take some time getting used to. Though, the real question was, now that she was free, what was she going to do?

While thinking about it, she pulled out her diary, dated it and wrote about her release. She wrote almost every day in her diary. It was in her diary where she found inner peace in being able to unleash her emotions on paper. She was also a very talented writer. Her stories were highly descriptive and emotional. She held nothing back. Whatever she felt came straight out of a pen.

She sat and wrote for almost an hour before deciding to go to a women's shelter that would take her in. She was given directions to a shelter about a mile away, which she walked to. Since she had no money, walking was the only option.

By the time she arrived, the place was crowded. There were all kinds of women waiting outside smoking and conversing. The name of the shelter was called, *Metrohouse.* JaQuita entered the building, requesting to speak to the person in charge of allowing her to stay. She was directed to an open bed where she could sleep. The mattress appeared old and dirty, yet it was something she could lay her head on. The woman in charge told her that dinner would be served in a couple hours, which was enough time for JaQuita to get situated and relax a little.

When dinner was finally served, she ate ferociously. She ate fast and was sure to collect seconds. It had been the best meal she had had in a very long time, since before going to prison. For dinner, she had meatloaf covered in gravy along with mashed potatoes, followed by a bowl of corn, a small side of salad and a bread roll. There was also fruit punch to drink. And if anyone had a sweet tooth, there were cookies and cupcakes available.

When dinner was over, she was instructed about the rules of the shelter. The maximum she could stay was four months from the time she entered. She was to be back every day by 6:30 p.m. or her bed would go to another person. She was told the times of each of the three daily meals. And of course, there was not to be any drugs or illegal activity in the shelter. If so, she was out immediately. That also went for any wild behavior or fighting. Apart from those restrictions, she was free to do whatever she wanted. She could come and go as she pleased.

On every Tuesday and Thursday, a pile of used clothes were delivered to the shelter, and any person could choose what they wanted. Whatever was left was thrown away, since that was the last stop of the donated clothes. JaQuita couldn't wait for that because she needed clothes. As a courtesy, one of the workers gave her a toothbrush, toothpaste and soap. JaQuita was grateful. After that, JaQuita slept for the entire night.

Over the next few days, JaQuita was able to collect a few clothes from the donation pile as promised. She now had three outfits that appeared decent. She even was able to collect a pair of tennis shoes to replace her old boots. There was a duffle bag that she found to carry her clothes in. She was sure to hand wash all her clothes before wearing them. Despite her ragged appearance, she was a clean woman.

During this time, JaQuita did nothing special. She would just walk long distances around the city, trying to get reacquainted with the world that she had left four years ago. She began to remember major street names and different areas of the city that she had gone to in the past. If she wasn't walking, she would sit on a city bench and write in her diary. Yet, she always made sure to be back to the shelter for every meal.

Within the week, she reported to the police station where she received an envelope with instructions on meeting her assigned parole officer. The first meeting was set up for Tuesday at 10 a.m., four days away. Yet rather than looking inside the envelope, JaQuita just took it and stuffed it in her pocket. She wasn't interested in knowing who her officer would be, since more than likely, she didn't know the person anyway.

On the way back to Metrohouse, JaQuita began wondering about her life and what she was going to do. Nothing had yet registered as far as goals were concerned. She wanted to live a life for the better. She had experienced so much in prison that she really wanted to take the opportunity to turn her life around in some way. She knew that it was better to live for good than to live for bad, and she wanted to live a life that was the direct opposite of her mother's. All that surrounded JaQuita throughout her childhood was abuse, neglect, betrayal, drugs, confusion and misguidance. In her heart, she didn't want that anymore. If only someone could come to her rescue and show her a better way, she would be so grateful. She hadn't really known how to live any better, but wanted to try now, since what she had chosen so far had not turned out so well.

When she arrived back at the shelter, she decided to skip dinner for a change. She just lay on her bed, staring at the ceiling—which had a few holes in it and hadn't been painted in a while—and just thought about her life. As usual, there was noise everywhere, but she was still able to contemplate things.

Over the next three days, JaQuita took to her regular routine, waiting for Tuesday to arrive so she could see her parole officer. That Monday evening, she finally took the paper out that she got a few days ago and looked at it. She was to report to the parole office, which was in a building that was a few blocks from the downtown police station. The parole officer she was assigned to was a woman named Mandi Harris. After reading that short detail, JaQuita folded it up, put it back in her pocket and dozed off to sleep.

3

Meet Mandi

JAQUITA APPEARED AT THE PAROLE OFFICE LOBBY THE following morning. It was the job of the parole officers to go to the lobby and call the names of those scheduled to meet them. However, Mandi had been on the phone and had asked her co-worker, Brandy, who had just walked past her office, to call for JaQuita. So when Brandy went out to call JaQuita's name, and JaQuita responded, she led her to Mandi's office. On the desk was a frame that read: Mandi Harris. Mandi's back was toward JaQuita as she shuffled through her file cabinet. Mandi was 37 years old at about 5'6 with a slender build. By her face, one would guess she was much younger. Her co-workers always recognized her to be happy all the time. She had a very youthful appearance and a smile that could light up any room, a demeanor that was not common among other parole officers.

"Aw, are you Mandi?" JaQuita asked.

Mandi turned. "I am," she smiled. "Just have a seat. I'll be right with you. I'm just digging for your file here."

JaQuita sat down and Mandi finally turned forward with the file in her hand. She then closed the cabinet, locking it with a key, and proceeded to sit in her chair.

As a native of Mississippi, she had a strong southern accent. "Yes, I am Mandi. I will be your parole officer for the duration of your parole, here. Now help me out, it's Jaa-kwee-ta… Jenkins. Correct?"

"Yes *ma'am*."

"OK. Now I hear you sometimes go by the name JJ, J, Jackie or just JaQuita. So which would you prefer I call you?"

"It don't matter," she said, shrugging her shoulders. "Whatever's cool wit'ch you is fine by me."

"Okay, well I'll just call you JaQuita, since that's your name," she smiled.

JaQuita just stared sideways, expressing no emotion whatsoever. In reality she wanted the whole session to be over with. Besides having to appear before Mandi periodically, what else could this woman possibly do for her, she thought. Mandi opened the folder, staring at JaQuita's record for a short while. She shifted back in her chair; then after a few minutes, began flipping pages in the folder before finally gathering herself together to begin her speech.

She read aloud to JaQuita her record. "Okaa-y," she began. "It shows here your name is JaQuita Queen Jenkins. Age, 23. You were born on June 5th 1970 at Venora Hospital in Detroit. Your mother is Brenda Jenkins. Father, unknown. You have no siblings. Oh… I'm sorry. It says here that your mom is now deceased. She died when you were 13. No family member elected to take care of you after her death. So the State later sent you to a foster home. You bounced around different foster homes until you were 18. You dropped out of Elmira High School during the 10th grade. You never went back to high school, nor obtained a diploma. You stayed with friends after you were 18. You have no children. *Alleluia*. At 19, you and a friend chose to rob a convenience store, during which the police later arrived, shooting your friend, I believe... whose name was Jodi, who is now deceased. You struggled and fought one of the officers, injuring him in the face, before eventually being taken down by other officers that were chasing you. With you, they found a knife. You were then taken into the County where you were later charged with armed robbery and aggravated assault, which you pled guilty to. The judge sentenced you to 5-7 years in prison but you only served four, at the Valerie State Correctional Facility. That was your first offence. It says also that you liked to drink and smoke. You like to smoke weed and indulge in pills such as Ecstasy and Xanax, which is why you tried to rob the store in the first place... so that you could get the money to buy those pills. It shows that while in prison, you liked to write and spend time alone. You're currently living in a shelter. You have no family or real friends to go to. However, you are finally getting a chance to experience what life is like on the outside since your first day in prison. How am I doing so far?"

"Uh... that's... that's pretty good," replied JaQuita, stunned by the details.

"Well... from this report, JaQuita, it appears that a woman like yourself is capable of anything. You can hurt anyone; perhaps even kill... if you have to. Therefore I am requiring that you meet with me as often as I say. You don't ever leave the county. You don't carry a gun or any concealed weapon. You don't do drugs unless prescribed by your doctor. You don't associate with any known felons or criminals. And you are not to take part in any criminal activity whatsoever, even if it's as small as stealing a toothpick. Now, you violate any of those rules, and expect to complete the rest of your time back at Valerie for up to three years along with any new charges you may have against you. Do I make myself clear? I mean, is there anything from what I just said that you don't understand?"

"No. Understood," replied JaQuita, softly.

Mandi then looked closely into JaQuita's eyes. She could sense the hurt and pain the young girl must have endured in the past, as with most former inmates. However, Mandi knew that there was more to a person than what was reported on file. Yet still as a parole officer, her job was to enforce the rules as she saw fit. However, something in her mind kept telling her to ask a more personal question.

"So... what are you going to do now with your life, JaQuita?"

"I'own know. Maybe find a job or somethin'."

"Listen, listen," Mandi began, slamming her desk. "When I'm talking to you, you look at me. Do you understand?"

JaQuita immediately sat up straight and looked her in the eye, before saying, "Yes, ma'am."

"I may not be old enough to be your mother, but you will respect me in my office," Mandi added.

Despite the fact that Mandi had a congenial and pleasant attitude, she was far from a pushover, and thus could speak her mind at anytime to anyone.

She then began. "Now I understand you're in an awkward state. You have no family to go to and you're all alone. And to you, I'm nothing more than a PO and I know things must be tough for you. I know there are a lot of uncertainties right now for you, but I am here to help if you want it. Mind you, that's *if* you want it."

JaQuita looked at her squarely and asked, "What could you possibly help me with? You don't know my life or what I've been through, except some short summary that you read in some folder... "

"I know. You're *right*. I don't know all you've been through. And I will be the first to admit it. I don't know. C'mon look at me," she pleaded. "I *don't* know. But what I *do* know is that in life, you have always two choices. You can either accept what life has given you so far and be pushed around as the victim, living a life of eventual destruction, which the system relishes... *or* you can change, which starts first with your mind. That means changing your attitude and the way you think, which will in turn change you as a person for the better, to eventual prosperity and success. Now that is what I know with all my heart to be true. One hundred percent. But the choice is yours."

JaQuita froze for a minute. No one had ever talked to her that way.

"Now JaQuita, I have been a parole officer for almost two years now. I became a school counselor before getting this job and unlike most parole officers, I care. I have seen a lot that can make your skin boil, and I say this to every former inmate that comes to my office. However, very few if any ever take my advice. Some do, but after they're done with me, I never hear from them again. For some of them, I've been the only family they've had. And coupled with endless cases of inmates I have to see, the work can be very frustrating and stressful, which is why the majority of the POs tend to not care anymore. It just becomes a job for another paycheck. Besides, we have our own families and challenges to worry about. Though I haven't been perfect, I still stood firm in my principles. I believe that if I can help one former inmate— even if it's just one—succeed from where they are now, then my life on earth was well worth it."

JaQuita was stunned. Never had she heard someone speak with such passion as Mandi did. She could sense the honesty in her voice. Suddenly she didn't want to leave her office.

"So what should I do?" she asked.

Mandi then glanced at her computer, before looking at the clock. "Well I have someone else I have to bring in since I'm on a tight schedule. However, I do want to give you an assignment to do that you can share with me if you want to. It's not an obligation, but if you want to share it with me, that's fine. But I believe it will be the first step in helping you find out what to do."

Mandi walked to the corner of her small office and pulled out a skinny green spiral notebook from a stack of notebooks she had and gave it to JaQuita. JaQuita took it and flipped through all the white pages that were all blank. It was a new notebook.

"What I want you to do is write down any and everything you want in life. It can be anything, like a car, clothes, a nice home, vacations, your own family, maybe a business or a job. Anything to your heart's content is fine. There's no limit. You can use as many pages as you want. It doesn't matter. You can also cut out pictures from magazines of the things you want and stick them to the pages. Then look at them and read them everyday until your next assigned visit. When you come back next time, you can share what you did… if you want to."

"Why, w-what's the point? I mean… "

"Do you want me to help you?" Mandi asked.

JaQuita nodded.

"Good. Then trust me on this. Now I have to bring in my next client. Remember it can be anything. Anything and everything."

"All right." JaQuita then stood up from the chair, and a small folded book suddenly sprung from the chair sideways onto the floor, which neither of them noticed. Without knowing how JaQuita would respond to a hug, Mandi chose to forgo it and escorted her back to the lobby and proceeded to call her next client as JaQuita left, staring at the notebook. However, before JaQuita could completely vanish, Mandi went over to her hastily to remind her of something she left out.

"Oh, and uh JaQuita?"

JaQuita turned. "Yes?"

"I forgot to tell you," she whispered, "Always use a blue pen whenever you write down your goals. Without going into too many details, it is more energetic for the mind and the universe."

JaQuita almost took a step back in total shock. She had never heard that before. "Really?" she thought. "Okay. No problem."

"All right. Now you take care." Mandi smiled, patting her on the back. "And remember… no more cases. Let's stay home this time."

JaQuita turned away lifting her hand in the air with the notebook, signaling that she understood. Mandi then turned around to look for her next case, a man named Brian Walker, who was standing right behind her.

"Alright. C'mon Brian," she said.

She escorted him to her office. When they got there, Brian noticed the folded book that was beside the chair and picked it up and placed it on Mandi's desk.

"What's this?" asked Mandi.

"I'own know. I jus' found it next to this chair, here."

Mandi glanced at the book. She picked it up and began looking through it. It contained several written paragraphs, like an essay paper. She flipped it around, before finally discovering that it belonged to JaQuita. It was her diary. Mandi began nosing through the diary as Brian waited in the chair. Some of the essays had dates written above them, which encompassed her whole time in prison. Mandi read a few short paragraphs that immediately drew her attention, but then caught herself and placed the book to the side of her work bag before finally attending to Brian. However, that day, JaQuita never returned to collect the diary, which Mandi was sure to read. Mandi knew that doing so was unprofessional, but she just couldn't help herself.

"Thanks, Brian," she said. It was all she could think of to say. However, Brian always liked to take advantage of any situation and compliment and asked a question that made both of them laugh.

"Does that mean now you'll get me off parole?" he asked.

4

❧❦

Secret Revelations

Mandi could not wait to read the diary. She had already read a lot of it during lunch and during another break at work. Rather than go home straight after work, she took a detour to the nearest library. Ronnie, her husband, was going to be there anyway along with their children: Honey, Daisy and Riley, ages 13, 10 and 8, respectively. And there would not be any more children after that, so Mandi thought. The theory was that once Ronnie finally got what he wanted, which was a boy, no more children were necessary, since they now had a taste of both worlds.

They were a happy family. The children respected each other and their parents. Occasionally, there were a few challenges like in all families, but at the end of the day, death was more preferred than any member leaving. Mandi enjoyed what she did and Ronnie, who was a construction worker, loved what he did. Their three children attended private schools, engaging in some extracurricular activities. Honey was a cheerleader, while Daisy played the piano. Riley, the youngest, played soccer. And together as a family, they would all volunteer at a local community center every once in a while. Not bad for a well-adjusted black family.

Sometimes, it still amazed Mandi how all those blessings came into her life. While a lot of women complained about their kids or families, Mandi was never a part of those conversations. She understood, having been a troubled youth herself, that all human beings are the creators of their experiences, and it is their thoughts and emotions that determine their destinies. It was a law—a law that can be measured at a quantum physics level. It was through this law that she was able to attain the home that she and Ronnie now owned, the loving husband she had, the adorable kids she gave birth to, the vibrant health that she had and so much more. All of this could only have been achieved using this law, as well as all she suffered through in the bad times. And it is a phenomenon that she instilled in her children, her husband—and anyone else who would listen. To her, *that* was the true key to changing the world. Everyone had to be exposed to this powerful, yet simple, law. And after reading some of JaQuita's diary, she believed it was her calling to help this young girl. It was Mandi's goal to aid a former inmate, and this was probably the one, after all these years of trying to reach people. Therefore, Mandi had to finish reading it.

As soon as she arrived at the library, Mandi immediately found the closest table, put her belongings down, took off her jacket, sat in the chair, grabbed the diary and read from where she left off. Some of the excerpts were redundant, but all the same, very powerful and chilling; none of them expressed much pleasure, but much pain. Pain from abuse. Pain from suffering.

Pain from neglect. Pain from lack of love. Just pain, pain, pain. And Mandi knew that whenever there was pain, one had to fill that hole with something else, which was usually the wrong thing for most troubled people, such as the drugs, alcohol, boys… anything to escape… as in JaQuita's case.

Though, it must be emphasized that JaQuita was a good writer. Everything she wrote was with specificity and intellect. It was almost surprising to witness such talent come from a young woman who was a high school drop-out. However while in prison, JaQuita passed the time away by trying to educate herself through reading books and writing, developing her gift.

One of her entries read:

Dear Diary,

If you look into my eyes, you will see pain and fear. Neither is dominant than the other. Last night my mom left the house with her boyfriend to have his way with me while she gets her fix. I'm only 11. Whenever she puts makeup on me, I know it's time. I try my best to feel nothing. I try my best not to cry. But I can't because of the pain. This is probably the third or forth time now. I never know what may happen. Everyday I'm alive is a gift. But what is the use of trying to make it. I do know there are better people in this world but I am unlucky. I am surrounded by chaos and endless nightmares. Misery is my only address. It is all I know; my world. Very little or no room is available to search for a better zip code. I want to cry for help, but who do I call? The cops? They're worse than the dealers themselves. I'm tired of the noise. I'm tired of the smells. I'm tired of being hungry. I'm tired of being angry.

I'm just so tired. I sometimes call for death to come, but it never shows up. I even try slitting my wrist so that it comes quicker, but I'm a coward. Take me away, take me away, oh death. At least I won't have to be tired anymore or feel the pain. I can rest now.

Another read:

Dear Diary,
Prison life is horrible. The commands, the food, and the people have all been another hell. Very few people have any remorse of what they've done. But it does show how little you are when you think you're tough out on the streets. The people are merciless. The guards don't care.

Anything can happen. Why is God keeping me alive this long is something I don't know. Since birth, I can't remember the last time I ever smiled. Again, misery is my only address.

Mandi kept reading until the library closed. She had just a few pages left, and she was so still-minded that it took her a while before she regained her focus on getting home. When she got home, she greeted her family.

"Honey what happened?" Ronnie asked. "It's almost 8:30."

"I know baby. I'm sorry, but today was just rough. That's all. I'm going to jump into the shower. I'm just so exhausted," she answered, without looking at him.

She went into the shower, dried off, and put on her gown before going to bed. She didn't even say "goodnight" to the kids. All she did was rest on the bed, staring at the ceiling, remaining still. What she read had stunned her into stillness. Everything was so revealing; so graphic. Ronnie, sensing his wife's estranged state, worried about what was going on.

Rarely did Mandi bring her work home with her. But tonight, she started to explain to her husband what had happened. She was so engaged in her thoughts that she didn't know when Ronnie drifted off to sleep. But Mandi couldn't sleep. She could decide not to worry about JaQuita, since it was not her problem. After all, JaQuita's story was not unlike all the other former parolees. However, she was involved now. So how could she ignore it? She was due to see JaQuita again in two weeks. All she could do was pray that JaQuita would do the exercise given to her.

But the diary did give Mandi an appreciation of how fortunate she was not to have experienced even a quarter of what JaQuita went through. How would she have taken it? What would she do? Although she, too, had her own share of battles and challenges earlier on as a child. And at that thought, Mandi drifted off to sleep.

Two weeks passed, and JaQuita was in the lobby awaiting Mandi.

"JaQuita Jenkins!" Mandi shouted.

It was a tone higher than normal. JaQuita rose up and approached Mandi. "Sorry for hollering," Mandi smiled frantically. "Uh, c'mon in."

When they arrived in the office, JaQuita sat down, while Mandi went over to her chair, giving JaQuita back her diary.

"Ah thanks, ma'am," JaQuita said happily. "I was looking all over for it. I was wondering where it was."

"No problem, but you don't have to call me ma'am. You can call me 'Mandi.' Mandi's fine."

"Okay, Mandi."

There was a slight pause. Then suddenly something came over JaQuita and she asked the question. "You didn't read this, did you?"

Mandi was not very good at lying. Her conscience wouldn't allow it. So she nodded slowly. "Listen, I'm sorry," she said as she approached JaQuita.

"But why? That's personal. You're not supposed to."

"I know, but… "

"You ain't supposed to read that. That's illegal." JaQuita's voice started to get loud, and then began to sound as if she was about to cry. Mandi tried to calm her down. She then hugged her, insisting that she lower her voice.

"Listen, you needed my help, right?" she asked. JaQuita nodded with her head in her lap. "Well... if I can't understand you, how can I reach you? Huh? How can I reach you?" she whispered. "How *can* I do it?"

JaQuita couldn't answer. "Now I want to help you. I promise everything we say will be strictly confidential. I will take it to my grave. You have my word. Just don't tell this to anybody. I know you suffered. You suffered a lot. But it's not your fault. You hear me. It's not your fault. And we are going to get through this, you and me. You hear me. I will do my best with what I know to help you, but don't you dare ever disrespect me in anyway, and we're cool. Deal?" JaQuita nodded.

"Good. Now as always, we have limited time. So let's hurry," she said as she scrambled to her chair. "Now did you write your list of things you want?"

"Yeah," JaQuita answered, holding the notebook in the air, flipping the pages.

Mandi was delighted. "Well, tell me just a few things you want. It doesn't have to be everything. Just something. Whatever you want to share is fine."

There was another slight pause. JaQuita then opened the notebook, a bit hesitant to read, but did. She began: "I wanna home of my own. I wanna a job... any job for right now. I wanna car... any car that works. I wanna have friends who are good to me."

Suddenly, she began to cry. Tears started pouring profusely down on her cheeks. She sniffed, trying to keep silent, but continued reading. "I want friends that love me. I... I wanna be married somed-day. I wanna... a... a husband... who will love me for me and is responsible. H-he won't hurt me or... beat me, or leave me, or cuss at me or... *spit* at me."

She tried again drying her eyes. "I wanna be happy. Free. I wanna be healthy and... drug free. I don't wanna be like my mother. I wa-ant... "

"Okay, that's enough. That's enough. You can stop now," Mandi interrupted, handing her a tissue. "Listen," she said, "I'm happy you did this exercise. Very few former inmates even do so. And I'm even happier you wrote with a blue pen. And look, you cut a picture of a Toyota car. Good job. But I want to say one important thing. Whenever you write your goals, don't ever put down things that you don't want to happen, such as 'he won't hurt me,' or 'spit at me,' because it stresses more of the opposite. Rather, put down 'I want a husband who's respectful, loving, honest, loyal… ' that sort of thing. Make sure all the characteristics are in the positive sense, okay?"

JaQuita nodded slowly. "Okay," she whispered.

Mandi then glanced at the clock and with a few seconds of thought made a decision.

"Now listen," she said. "I will give about 10 minutes of my time to educate you on a powerful law that you will need to exercise every day of your life to obtain everything in that book that you wrote, *if* you really want it. Along with this speech are going to be books that I recommend you read that will further educate you and help you understand this law and how the universe really works. Okay?"

JaQuita nodded anxiously.

"Now please remember, this is not my job. Nor am I getting anything out of it. I just want to do this because it was passed onto me, and in order for valuable information to ever be kept, it must be shared. You got it?"

"I got it."

"Now, the best way to start off explaining this is by telling you that we are all connected by a very special law in the universe. It is the most powerful law in the world. It is called the law of attraction. Without getting into too much detail, I will say this, the law of attraction is a principle that states that like things attract other like things in this universe. Therefore, whatever you think about most of the time, you attract.

Thoughts are physical things and the things which you are thinking about, come into your existence in time. They must. It's a law. Therefore, what you wrote down, you can get. But you have to believe it whole heartedly, because it is only doubt that will cause it not to come into your life."

"But how do I get these things?" JaQuita retorted.

"Ah hah," Mandi smiled. "The 'how' is not important. In fact, it really is irrelevant. You don't have to worry about the 'how.' All you have to know is that you're going to obtain whatever you're seeking, and in someway somehow, the 'how' will find a way to make that thing that you want obtainable... usually when you least expect it. But again, you must truly believe in it first, in order for it to work."

"Bu... but how will it do that, though?" JaQuita asked eagerly, trying to make sense of it all.

"I'm glad you asked. The law of attraction will attract things that you desire through placing situations, events, people, and other variable scenarios you can't determine or imagine, into your life that will cause you to obtain that which you desire. You see, your brain is working 24/7 and from that powerful machine are thoughts that you think of everyday that send signals, or frequencies, or energy to all parts of the globe to match that which you're thinking, which to the universe, is what you want. No matter how big or small the thought is, it will operate to your command. It will move mountains, cut through steel, plow through oceans, valleys, hills, and beyond, shifting things around to see that you get it. There is virtually no limit in obtaining that which you seek. Those things will come into your existence through the law of attraction. It *is* the most powerful law in the universe; more powerful than the law of gravity or anything you can think of. Therefore, whenever you apply it, all other things become second-class. And once you master this law and understand it, life will be so magical and breathtaking; you will enjoy every minute of it."

Suddenly a big smile lit up JaQuita's face, and a sudden sensation of new understanding. She remembered saying a prayer to God, asking for her life to be changed, and now was the start of a new chance. Was this the law of attraction Mandi was referring to? She was ready to find out.

"Well, how do I use this law of attraction or this… this energy?"

"Sweetheart, you've been using this power ever since you were born. The only thing is that you've been using it the wrong way. You've been focusing too much on what's going wrong in your life. And therefore, you're experiencing more of the pain. You see, the law of attraction will give you whatever you think and feel on a consistent basis, whether good or bad, because it responds strictly to your thoughts and feelings. No questions asked. It has been tested and studied by many scientists. Men like Albert Einstein and Thomas Edison all confirmed this through their studies. Your mind is a powerful weapon that is the most sacred and limitless creation ever known to man."

"So what do I do?!" JaQuita asked excitedly. She suddenly became fascinated with the subject and was eager to know more.

"Well first of all, I want to make it clear. You have tremendous baggage. Lots and lots of baggage. Therefore, the techniques are not going to be executed perfectly overnight. I mean, you won't get everything you listed tomorrow. The things you wrote in your diary expressed nothing more than pain. And when you express pain like that, you are sending more signals to the universe to bring more painful experiences into your life. You need to first of all heal, love yourself more, and become happier and excited. Also, you must throw that diary away and replace it with pleasurable experiences. Understand that God made you right. There is nothing wrong with you. You are a beautiful and attractive creation. You need to start feeling good right now. That means feeling anything that is in correlation with joy. It could be singing, dancing, smiling, feeling confident, secure, worry free—anything that is similar to the feeling of joy."

Mandi then looked at her clock. She was a little past the 10-minute marker. "Now listen, I can't discuss this further with you, but believe me, I would. I love talking about this subject and could go on for hours. But here, I have a list of things that I typed in the past which you can do in order to feel good. Remember, the key first is to always feel good because that is when you know you're on the right track to achieving what you want. When you have that feeling, it is then when the universe will direct your thoughts to things you want, since it is matching those things that make you feel good." She then handed JaQuita a list of exercises she could do to feel good.

"Also another thing," Mandi added. "I don't know how adamant you are on reading, but it is real important, especially as it is related to this subject. Even if it's a page a day, it does wonders to your mind in establishing more aspirations and ideas. Now I will give you one book. I want it back once it's completed. It's called *The Magic of Thinking Big* by David Schwartz.

It doesn't deal completely on the law of attraction, but it helps in developing you from the inside out in becoming a better person because the first step, like I mentioned before, is changing your attitude. Then you change how you think, talk, act, dress, smell and so forth. This is what starts the process of you gaining respect from others and making you feel good inside, which is the beginning of the attraction process. I have a list of other books which I hope you will read, but let's see how you do with this one first."

"Lovely," JaQuita replied. "Thank you."

"And lastly, you're going to have to make some new friends. This is a new path for you, so you want to protect it with positive people. Just remember this, 'If you want things in your life to truly change, you're going to have to truly change things in your life.' When millionaires get together, who do they usually, if not always, associate with?"

"Mu-millionaires?"

"Exactly. That's because they understand energy and know that you become who you surround yourself with." Mandi then glanced again at the clock. "Okay, now you got to go, *now*. We'll continue in two weeks. Make sure you got everything," she spoke as she started directing JaQuita out of her office.

JaQuita collected everything, both books and papers. She then scrambled out, fumbling a bit with what she was carrying. All the same, she was excited. She just could not wait to read and digest all this knowledge. To her, this was heaven-sent. It truly was the miracle she had prayed for!

Over the next two weeks, JaQuita became engrossed in the law of attraction. She could not sleep the entire night following her last meeting with Mandi. She began imagining more and more and it became more apparent to her that she had the power. She began adjusting her dreams in her goal book a little more to meet specificity. But she was not perfect, she did still engage in a little drinking. She still smoked cigarettes, had not made new friends yet, and conversed with friends of old. However, she refused weed when offered, especially since that would be a parole violation, and she limited her exposure to bad influences.

There were no late nights or major outings; just chit chat. When she was not doing that, she was either reading *The Magic of Thinking Big* or studying different exercises to keep her spirits high. She eventually disposed of her old diary. It was a good detailed writing tool, but it was almost too easy to throw away, for she wanted nothing to remind her of her painful past.

Besides, the list exercise Mandi gave JaQuita to do would occupy enough of her time. The exercise was called *The Dos to Feeling Good*. She was to find at least five things she could do on a regular basis in order to feel good. It was virtually impossible for JaQuita her to limit her things to just five.

The Dos to Feeling Good list read like this:

Hiking	*Drawing*
Walking	*Writing*
Playing your favorite music	*Exercising (e.g.: biking, swimming, fencing, etc.)*
Dancing	*Yoga*
Getting Reiki	*Laughing*
Cooking	*Smiling*
Planting in a garden	*Hugging someone*
Getting a pet	*Painting/pottery*
Getting a massage	*Something in arts and crafts*
Playing a Musical Instrument	*Singing*

Then below, was a short list of exercises that were considered very necessary to do. It was designed to help the overall health of the body in order to strengthen the physical body, making it better to spiritually and energetically support what JaQuita wanted.

They were:

Get a cleanse in all these areas of the body: colon, gall bladder, liver and pancreas

Get a Candida yeast cleanse along with a fat cell cleanse

Eat organic fruits and vegetables or foods that are as close as nature intended

Eat grains or fiber (e.g.: oatmeal, organic bread, buckwheat, etc.)

Drink all natural spring water

From the first list, JaQuita chose to write, walk, and a few others. With writing, she was going to document only positive aspects of the day, even if it was as small as waking up in the morning. As for the other list, she realized all those activities would require money. Therefore she decided she would engage in them once she found a job. As for Mandi and her family, they did all of this on a consistent basis.

JaQuita soon decided to remove her braids and finally wash her hair. She then brushed it to make it appear straighter and firm. She also washed her clothes and developed better hygiene habits. She bathed and brushed her teeth daily. Her added confidence enabled her to look herself in the mirror. She studied her face. She would make different gestures and appearances intended to appear joyous. Was it her imagination or was she starting to actually feel more joy and love herself?

And it was then she began laughing, then crying. Whether they were tears of joy or tears of pain, was unclear. All that was clear, was that this was a new transformation from the old JaQuita. She had made the decision to change and there was no going back. Whatever old habits she still had would eventually be resolved later, she felt.

Within one week, she finished *The Magic of Thinking Big*. She loved it! Never had she read a book of its kind. She had underlined and highlighted sentences and paragraphs throughout the book. The next thing she did with the information was to write it down on a separate sheet of paper so that she could refer back whenever she wanted. Since the book wasn't hers, she wanted to remember all the key elements. She was that committed to change—like a student. And just knowing that made her feel proud. She was just so eager to learn more. Out of all these actions, she felt pleasure and relief from almost everything.

Nothing seemed to hurt as before. It was as if 10 dump trucks were finally lifted from her shoulders. That's how much weight negativity can have on a person. Is it any wonder why people get tired so easily? The stress, at least most of it, just started to leave JaQuita. And that definitely felt good. But it must be made clear: This was a decision that she made on her own. A lot of people who Mandi consulted with made it seem complicated. JaQuita understood easily, that by changing your mind and feelings, you change your destiny. Period. End of story.

During her next meeting, Mandi surprised her with a urine cup, for her urine to be sampled. JaQuita understood without flinching. She was so occupied with what she was doing that marijuana was the last thing on her mind. Mandi could feel that energy, which was why she wasn't worried either. It was just protocol.

When JaQuita returned the book to Mandi, she was given another, called *How to Win Friends and Influence People* by Dale Carnegie. This was another classic that highlighted the fundamentals to developing a good personality and the secrets to being liked by other people. This was going to be so valuable to JaQuita because she had been prone to trying to fit in and making people like her no matter the cost. Ever since her mother was gone, she yearned for anyone's attention. Therefore she went through drastic measures to be liked, which would explain why she slept with different boys throughout high school. But with this book, she didn't have to do that anymore.

"So how long has this 'law of attraction' been known?" she asked Mandi.

"Since the beginning of time," she answered.

She then added, "The law of attraction has been known for several centuries by all ancient rulers, such as pharaohs, emperors, generals, great kings, queens, presidents, people of high offices, and members of royal families. Basically this law… or I should say, this secret, has been something that has been only shared among members of the elite so that they could keep the power amongst themselves, and enslave everyone else, thus maintaining all the control and free choice for themselves."

"So that's why it is not known by many people," JaQuita commented.

"Exactly."

"Because I asked some people if they knew 'bout the law of attraction and none of them had the slightest clue what I was talking about."

"Of course not, and the ones that do, will deny it. Simply put: The rich don't want competition. Just think about it this way. Imagine how the world would be if everyone in the world had abundance and was free. Just think about it. There would be no weapons, no war, no famine, no crimes, no police, no court system, no prisons, no DEA, state, federal, or local regulations... "

"But wouldn't you be out of a job?" JaQuita replied immediately.

Mandi paused for a second, and then spoke. "Yes. I wouldn't be working here, but due to my abundance, I would be channeling my energies to something else. Remember since I also have abundance, I and everyone else with it, would be contributing to a better planet—a better world."

JaQuita stood silent for a minute. Never had she thought of it that way.

Mandi then continued on. "Right now, you should concentrate first on making yourself better in character. Now that doesn't mean you're not already perfect in God's eyes. As people, we all have areas for improvement. It's a never ending process. But based on your past, you need to form a habit of a better attitude. Since you're trying to change how you've been behaving in the past, this is all new to you. So you have to continue on that path until it becomes fully ingrained in your subconscious. It has to be an attitude you have to perform without thinking about it; kind of like knowing your own name."

"Well then how do I get to that level?"

Mandi had never gotten so far with a former inmate, and thus had never been asked this. So she paused for a moment. "Mmmm… try to feel good for the next 21 days and it will become a habit—like brushing your teeth," she answered.

"Okay, but I have another question. How can I avoid thinking negative thoughts? Because sometimes, it's hard. I mean… "

"Say no more," Mandi smiled. "I'm glad you asked that. While the law of attraction starts with your thoughts, the real power behind it comes from your feelings. You know what it's like to feel good, now, don't you?"

JaQuita nodded.

"Well, the key is to feel good always, because as long as you feel good, the negative thoughts just aren't there. And besides, don't worry about every thought you think about. Researchers state that we think over 60,000 thoughts a day, but it's our feelings that make all the difference. And remember, what matters is consistency. One negative thought won't do it. One positive thought won't do it. Overall, it's how you are the most of the time that will make the difference. That's why I had you make a list and have pictures of all the things you want. That way, you can look at it all the time, helping you stay consistent in your ambitions."

"Wow… I never knew that."

"You see JaQuita, if there is one thing I would like for you to take with you, it is this: You have the power to change your life. You see, your mind is your own genie. You determine your destiny. You determine your future because you are creating that future through your own thoughts, and those thoughts are yours. You are free to think whatever you want. Another great man by the name of Earl Nightingale said this, 'The strangest secret is that we become what we think about most of the time.'"

This made JaQuita so excited. The thought that she had this much power over her destiny was like music to her ears.

"I want you to know that it does not matter your background, where you came from, or who you are because the universe can't tell the difference. All it does is respond to your thoughts and emotions. That is why it's important to know that it isn't the tough economy, or the government, or the police, or the fancy school you never went to, or the father you never knew, or the mother you had. No one or thing is to blame for you not becoming successful in life. Whatever has been the outcome of your life today, you created it… through your own thoughts and feelings. No one is to blame but you. You just didn't know it before."

That was a tough pill for JaQuita to swallow, which had her suddenly moving and twisting her body in anguish.

"But now that you know, the blessing is that you can do something about it," Mandi added. "You have to execute this power consistently, everyday. Wang Yangming, who was a Chinese philosopher during the 16th century, said this, 'To know and not to do, is not to know.' Think about it."

Mandi then glanced at the clock again. "Well that will be all the lessons for today. Don't forget to drop your urine. I also want to give you *The Do Not Do List*. This list comprises of all the things you must not do while working this technique. They affect your thoughts and emotions, which is why you should avoid them at all times as much as possible. They are not healthy for your body… at all, which can delay or eliminate what you really want to come into your life."

She handed JaQuita the list and then escorted JaQuita out of the office, reminding her to come back at the same time in two weeks.

5

~~~⟨⟩~~~

Tears of Joy

JaQuita was a bit uneasy from the *Do Not Do List*. Included in it were things she had been used to doing before prison, and to finally give them up was a challenge. She enjoyed Xanax and Percocet. However, she believed avoiding them was the solution to achieving her goals. According to her, Mandi hadn't lied to her thus far. Also, she kept remembering the one statement Mandi made, which was: *If you want things in your life to truly change, you're going to have to truly change things in your life.* Also, it was apparent that she had to get better friends than the ones she had. She was on the positive road for greatness. If she wanted to stay on course, how could she possibly associate with people who were on a negative path? It's like oil and water. The two just don't mix.

Coupled with this, JaQuita was in search of a job, and possibly her own place. To her, having her own place would be the key to focusing solely on herself and her goals, without being distracted by the noisy housemates in the shelter. So she made sure to put that among her goals in the notebook. Whatever she wanted, she wrote down.

She also listed that she wanted a job. She wasn't really concerned with the type of job, provided she could work. But, based on the fact that she was a parolee with two felonies, the odds weren't that good. However there was one thing Mandi pointed out to her earlier, which was this: *When your behavior's right, the facts just don't count.* That message stuck with her. Basically, it meant that despite all the odds of a goal not being attained, the universe will find a way to make it a reality, provided the person stays positive. So JaQuita stayed as positive as she could, hopeful that some way, somehow, things would work out.

Under the *Do Not Do List*, it read:

Do not eat pork
Do not eat shellfish
Do not eat any food containing high fructose corn syrup, dextrose, or sucralose
Do not eat any food containing monosodium glutamate, MSG
Do not take any vaccinations, even a flu shot
Do not take any prescription or non-prescription drugs
Do not indulge in diet sodas or artificial sweeteners
Do not eat or drink any products containing aspartame
Do not apply creams on your body that contain mineral oil
Do not use anything containing fluoride
Do not get a root canal

According to Mandi, any application of these things would affect a person's thought process and how she felt, which would in turn cause an inability for the person to transmit signals effectively.

Whenever the condition of the mind or body is not at ease, the energy sent from the brain, will always be low or less frequent, which would in turn cause whatever object or desire not to manifest properly. And it is great intensity and frequency that is required for the energy of the universe to bring any wishes to light. JaQuita also wrote down that she wanted to be healthy; thus meaning becoming a non-smoker and ridding herself of any other habits that would fall under the category of *unhealthy living*. She had been smoking since the age of 12, but knew that she had to quit. She wanted to quit and live healthy. The same applied for alcohol.

She didn't want to ever touch a bottle again. But the cravings appeared unconquerable. Still, she wrote it down. As for pills, she believed she could kick that habit as well. The key was for her to stay away from people who engaged in that activity. That's when it finally dawned on her: All of this could be totally eliminated if she distanced herself from Peanut and her friends. They were close friends with Jodi, the girl she went with to rob the food store. JaQuita now wanted no part in their lives, but without a mother or relatives, they were really the only family she had. This came as a problem for JaQuita. Yet, she kept it simple. She wrote in her goal book to have positive friends, and left it up to the universe to decide how that would happen.

She also was careful about staying in touch with how she felt. So she took every day at a time, monitoring her emotions, remembering to feel good always. It wasn't to feel good only when convenient, or when something good happened. The key was to feel good always. When she wasn't doing that, she continued reading and conducting a few of the exercises from the To Do List.

Over the next week, JaQuita went around the city to restaurants, gas stations, stores, department stores and libraries, looking for a job. She completed 22 applications. The following week, she met with Mandi. The conversation was per usual. Mandi asked for her comments on what she read, as well as answered any questions JaQuita had. She had already finished the last book, *How to Win Friends and Influence People*. This time, Mandi gave her two more books, titled, *The Power of Positive Thinking* by Norman Vincent Peale and *The Magic of Believing* by Claude M. Bristol.

The first book mostly dealt with emotions and how character defines a person's fate in life in such a logical pattern. JaQuita was definitely going to enjoy the book and understand more about the concept. The meeting was not as long as it usually was, but all the same, JaQuita took in as much as she could from Mandi.

The other book by Claude Bristol exemplified the power of belief and how profound of an impact it has on reality. In it was example after example of people in the past who were successful, which confirmed the validity and the power of this new law she had been learning about. In fact, it was reported that it was that particular book that propelled Liberace to success in entertainment, as well as Arnold Schwarzenegger.

Within a few days, JaQuita was halfway through the first book. She decided to go to the library to collect magazines that contained pictures that matched her needs. For instance, if she grabbed a magazine on finance or business, she would look for pictures of cash or gold and cut them out. If it was a fashion magazine, she looked for pictures of famous designer clothes. If it was a magazine on vehicles, she looked for luxury cars and would cut them out. If it was a fitness magazine, she'd cut out pictures of attractive male models as her ideal mate. After she collected all the pictures from those magazines, she taped them inside her goal book to look at them as often as possible. To her, it was just fun, but also interesting to see whether this power really worked.

One important thing Mandi remembered to emphasize clearly to JaQuita was that she had to give all her dreams time to manifest. She emphasized that the law of attraction is working in perfect speed to deliver the items she wanted, based on her level of belief. The number one reason why people failed in achieving their dreams was because they focused on things they had little or no belief in acquiring, then they wondered why they weren't coming into their lives. Also, they put too much emphasis on how those desires would all come together.

Mandi told JaQuita that if she would only concentrate on the goals she had a strong belief in acquiring, then those dreams would come much faster than the ones she didn't believe in. No dream was too big or too small for the law of attraction to bring into one's existence. However, its manifestation was dependent on one's own belief level.

In JaQuita's case, she strongly believed in getting a job and having a place of her own. She believed the universe would provide the sole mate of her dreams. She believed in becoming free of cigarettes, alcohol and drugs. She believed that she would have positive friends. She believed that she could own a car. She strongly believed in all of these things. But if you were to ask her whether she believed she could own a Mercedes, the answer was "no." So, in her case, Mandi would tell her not to concentrate on that goal for right now.

Mandi also explained that the "how" was irrelevant. She said that millions upon millions of different variables were being calculated by the energy of the universe to decipher the best situation to bring her particular desires, all of which could not be determined by any man on earth. The universe knows man better than man knows himself.

Therefore, it knows at what time and at what place is perfect for a person to receive that desire, since it is going according to one's own feelings and thoughts. Therefore figuring out how it would all happen was a waste of time. The law of attraction has already made the calculation. All she had to do was feel good about it and believe that it was on its way, and she would get it.

When JaQuita heard this, she was a little agitated, because like most people, she wanted them right now. However, she hoped she would see and recognize some results in order to believe that this entire phenomenon existed. Her biggest desire was to get a job. A couple more weeks passed and it was apparent that all 22 applications were denied. Either the employers weren't hiring at the moment or recognized she was an ex-con.

Then, on her way back to *Metrohouse*, shortly after receiving all these rejections, she recognized a restaurant that she hadn't visited yet. It appeared Italian and family owned. On the window was the big sign, saying, "Now Hiring." She stood still for a moment, staring at it. Now she had already seen over a dozen different signs with the same display. However, this was different. The more and more she stared at the store, the more drawn she felt to applying. She didn't know what they served or any of the people in there. All she knew was that some *thing* was suggesting that she go in. So she did.

When she entered, she was approached by a young man at the counter. "Can I help you?" he asked.

"Oh yeah. I was… I mean, I saw you guys were hiring."

"Oh the job? Yeah, let me get you an application." He went to a small room to get the form before returning back. "Now we're looking for a waitress. Can you do that?" he asked.

"Sure," JaQuita replied.

"Good. Just sit down, fill that out, and we'll let you know once you're done."

JaQuita sat at a nearby table. There were some customers present with a jukebox playing in the background. Before she reached halfway through her application, the young man appeared to her again. "Listen, we're really low on staff. Can you come in next Thursday at 2:30?" he asked.

JaQuita smiled. "Certainly. I can come in at that time," she said.

"All right, good. The person you should ask for is Pacco, okay? He's the owner. He'll just ask you a few questions, give you a tour… that kind of thing, then you should be all set with your uniform and everything."

"*Okay,*" she replied.

After she completed the application, she gave it to the man. "By the way, what's your name?" JaQuita asked him.

"Georgio. I'm the owner's nephew," he said shaking her hand.

"Okay well thank you, Georgio."

"No. Thank *you.* Just remember, next Thursday at 2:30. Don't be late. He hates that."

"Thanks. I won't."

JaQuita left the restaurant. She was so excited. She had never felt that way about the other places she applied at. A part of her just knew she had already gotten the job. She was beginning to believe how this all made sense. Slowly, her dreams were manifesting.

The following Wednesday came. JaQuita was walking down the street from the shelter, when suddenly a car pulled up right in front of her, nearly frightening her to death.

"Yo, what up bitch! Wha's happenin'? Y'own remember me? It's yo girl, Peanut. Remember?"

JaQuita took a second, then recognized her. "Oh what up? How's it going?" she asked enthusiastically. They then gathered and hugged.

"We heard you was out, so we said, 'let's holla at ya'"

"Cool, cool. I can dig it. So who dis wit'ch you?" JaQuita asked.

"Oh… in the car is Liz. You remember Liz don't'ch you, from ninth grade? She had a little baby. His name's Dexter. He's 3. Say 'hi' Dexter," she signaled to him. "Then in there, is my lil' sister Desiray, and in the passenger seat is Anthony, my boyfriend. So don't mess with him! He's mine! Ya undastand?" She laughed. "Ya know I'm just kiddin'. So anyway, what's up with you? I heard you's at the Metrohouse for now. So I just figured we come by. You come ride with us, have a few drinks, smoke some weed. Take a few *pills*. You know we got that good shit you like. Ya know? Then we can hang a lil' bit. Kick it. You know, chill. Relax. I'l jus' be like ol' times. What ya say? You know I jus' wanna welcome you back."

JaQuita looked at the car. In it were open alcohol bottles and clouds of smoke everywhere. "W-Where would I sit?" she asked.

"Ah, it ain't shit," Peanut retorted. "Liz'll put Dexter on her lap and you can then squeeze yo' tight lil' ass over there, right between her and Desiray. By the way, you done lost a lot of weight, *girl*. We need ta fatten you up a lil' bit."

JaQuita looked and paused, feeling speechless. Her heart was not willing to go with them. She really didn't want to do anything with them. But a part of her didn't want to abandon them entirely, since they were part of her family; people she spent the most of her time with before she went to prison. But she sincerely knew they were bad news.

"I-I-I can't," she said.

"Well, why not?"

"Because… I-I just ca-an't. You know I… "

"Know what? Uh? Know what? I mean we knew each other since the third grade. So don't be going soft on me now. You lucky I'm here because we almost the only family you got. Jodi's dead and them other two, got less than a year left. So who you got left? Your mother… "

"Don't you say shit about my mother," she retorted back, pointing at Peanut. "You understand me? Don't you ever… You don't know shit. You hear me?"

Suddenly JaQuita stooped downward almost as if she was about to cry. Peanut's voice suddenly became softer. "Listen, all I'm sayin' is for you to kick it with us. We'd love to have you back. I know you on parole and shit, but you ain't gone catch no case with us, *baby*. C'mon."

Suddenly JaQuita rose up and glanced at her and said, "I can't. All right?" Then she proceeded to walk away.

Peanut then looked at her in dismay. "Well then fuck it then, bitch. Fuck you! I wish you stayed in jail! And don't you ever come to my house again. Don't ask to sleep over as you always did, or get something to eat. You hear me bitch?! Because you ain't getting' shit! Let's see how you make it with out me, you selfish bitch!"

"Yeah, fuck you," added Desiray.

"Biatch" added Liz as well.

JaQuita then turned and yelled to them, "Not one of you wrote me a single letter when I was locked up, or came to visit me."

However they continued to curse her out, before eventually driving off. JaQuita was relieved.

Thursday finally came. JaQuita was so excited as she prepared for the new job she believed she was getting. She needed to take two busses to get there and had the all-day pass ready to go. Her style was clean. She brushed her hair smooth and put on some perfume. She put just a touch of lipstick to her bottom lip, smacked them both, looked in the mirror, smiled, and was ready to go. She looked beautiful, too. Any meaningful man with a pulse would want to get to know her.

She hopped on the first bus, slid the pass through the machine and went to the back. A few minutes into the ride she heard a conversation between two men sitting together. One was reading the paper while the other one was talking next to him. Now nothing at all was peculiar about any of that, except for what was being said.

"You know that was really messed up. And it says here that the little boy was only 3," said one of them, reading the paper.

"Wow," replied the other.

"Yeah I know and all three of the girls were… including that guy who was in the passenger seat. Beer was just everywhere. Go figure. That's must be what happens when you drink and drive. And… and none of them had a seatbelt on."

JaQuita was listening word for word through the entire conversation, feeling a bit tensed and uneasy. "Excuse me, sir. Can I please see that paper?" she asked one of the men.

The man holding the paper turned and stared down at her for a moment. "Sure. Just one moment," he said.

The man then folded all the papers together in one big pile and gave them to her.

"Thank you," she said.

"Sure. No problem."

Before she was through reading the first two sentences, JaQuita was in tears. It was Peanut and the rest of the group she saw the day before. They had all been killed instantly by oncoming traffic. According to the paper, the driver, who was Peanut, lost control of the wheel, intoxicated, and was hit sideways by two oncoming vehicles. The two cars tried to stop, but not soon enough to avoid the collision. This hit JaQuita like a ton of bricks. She didn't have the strength to even stand up. Some other passengers on the bus came over to comfort her. It was apparent to them that she knew the people killed. A few moments later, JaQuita regained focus. The newspapers were scattered everywhere. And tears were all over her face.

She now needed to fix herself up before the interview. But there was one problem: She was now way past the stop she needed to get off at, in order to connect to the next bus that went to the restaurant.

She started to pull the cord repeatedly. As soon as the next stop came up, the bus stopped and she rushed out. She began turning in circles asking herself what she had done wrong. It was apparent now that she was going to be late. The closest estimate of the time she could get to the restaurant by was 3 p.m. if she took the next bus.

She was disoriented and confused. She wanted that job so bad and now it seemed over. She did not know what to do. She wanted to cry, but it seemed she had already done enough of that on the bus. She then became frantic and went to a nearby bench and began sobbing again, looking down at the pavement.

"This shit doesn't work. This shit doesn't work," she kept saying aloud. "I tried, but this doesn't work... AT ALL!"

"What doesn't work?" replied a voice.

JaQuita looked around to see who that was, and right in front of her stood a young black man, looking straight at her. "Huh?" she asked.

"I should be asking you," the young man smiled.

Just then, JaQuita began sniffing, drying her eyes, and fixing her collar rapidly as if a drill sergeant was right before her.

"Oh, hi," she said, trying to smile. "That was nothing. I just you know was... trying... to... I mean... "

"Listen, that's all right. You don't have to explain. By the way, my name's Eriq... with a Q," he said, extending his hand.

"JaQuita," she replied, shaking his hand with her own that was all covered in tears. "Oh, I'm sorry," she said, suddenly recognizing.

"It's all right," he smiled. "Here, I have a handkerchief. Take it and dry your face."

She took it and dried her face quickly. "Blow your nose if you have to. Don't be scared," he suggested. JaQuita did so, wiping her nose fully.

"I work at a gym and often we use towels or handkerchiefs to wipe off sweat from the machines. And I have plenty of clean handkerchiefs that I took along with me, so don't worry about it."

"Aw, thank you," replied JaQuita.

"No problem. So tell me. Are you lost? Did you lose a boyfriend? I mean what's going on?" JaQuita laughed.

"I like that smile," he added.

"Oh thanks. No, what it was, was that I knew the people that were killed in that car crash."

"Oh wow. I heard about that. That must have been awful."

"Yeah, we were close. I mean the driver and her sister were close to me. I didn't know the guy or anything."

"Oh wow. I'm sorry to hear about that."

"It's okay," replied JaQuita.

There was then a slight pause.

"Well… I can't bring the dead back to life but I would like to interest you to a cup of coffee. Maybe that might ease your pain a little bit."

"Are you serious?" JaQuita asked.

"Yeah, I just got off of work and could sure use the company… especially with a nice looking thang like yourself. C'mon I won't bite. I promise."

"You work close by?"

"Yeah, I'm a fitness instructor at the local gym down the street there. It's called Ruder Fitness. You may have heard of it. Anyway, I help mentor people on how to stay in shape. We had our usual staff meeting which occurs once a month between 10 and noon. Therefore, we never ever finish at this time. We're usually done before one o'clock. But this time, our boss had some family emergency he had to attend to and had us wait at the gym until he got there. We of course got paid, but still we waited for a long time. It's just now we got out."

JaQuita was amazed. Could this actually be true? Is this how the universe really worked? Does the law of attraction work like this… this fast? If so, oh law of attraction, do your work, she thought. After all, he fit the descriptions of the male models whose pictures she had cut out and put in her dream book. So all she could do was smile in astonishment.

"What? What's so funny? *Huuuuh*?" he asked, bumping her slightly.

"Oh nothing." JaQuita glanced at her watch. There was now no way she could possibly make her appointment on time. And besides, she no longer cared. The man beside her was suddenly more important than anything else at this moment.

"I would be honored to have that cup of coffee with you," she said with enthusiasm.

"Well all right. It's just this café across the street. Are you on a time schedule or anything?"

"No. I'm not. I have plenty of time."

"Good."

As they approached the café, Eriq opened the door for her and the two sat at a nearby table that was next to the front window. It was there they continued their conversation. The name of the place was called *The Soul Café*. Eriq had a good sense of humor. He was a light skinned man with a slender build at a height of 5'11, age 26. He grew up in a Baptist family. His mother was a librarian and a choir director for their church, while his father lived on disability benefits as a result of an injury suffered from one of the auto plants he had worked at for over 20 years. Yet, he volunteered his time as mentor to a youth group for disadvantaged children. Eriq's parents had been married for 27 years. He had a younger brother named Justin who attended Michigan State University, studying civil engineering. He was a senior.

The story of Eriq was that of a young man who seemed to always be outgoing since he was a child. Throughout grade school, he was athletic. He ran track, played basketball and baseball. Though his true talent was in baseball. In high school, he became an exceptional player, finishing with a batting average of .341, 9 home runs, and 8 stolen bases his senior year. During that same year, his team won the Division II state baseball championship. As a result of his excellence, he attained a Division I scholarship to the University of Michigan. He continued to excel in college baseball, which had some experts predicting he would one day enter the major leagues. He was best known for his base hits and spectacular catches in the outfield.

However, midway through his junior season, he shattered his right knee while rushing for home plate during extra innings. His team won the game, but the injury later proved fatal to his career. After two surgeries and months of rehab, the knee was just never the same. So with not knowing what else to do, Eriq went back home and found a job working at a gym before becoming a certified fitness instructor. He enjoyed health and wellness and modeled his personal behavior after those interests. He ate healthy and always exercised. His diet consisted of organic foods and he took daily vitamin supplements.

He had a son named Preston. He was 5 years old and was the love of Eriq's life. However, Eriq wasn't married. The child's mother was a woman Eriq had dated in college. Sophia was also a student at the time, and that was probably the nicest thing anyone could say about her. Throughout their time together, Sophia was never monogamous. She would flirt and play games with any man she felt was worth her time, which was why, when she became pregnant, Eriq denied being the father. But when the test results returned, they concluded the opposite. Anyone who knew Sophia and Eriq knew that Eriq made a horrible decision picking Sophia as a mate. Yet that was the problem with Eriq. He always made poor decisions when it came to choosing women.

When the child was born, however, it didn't change Sophia's character. She would still go out to clubs and rarely take care of the baby or provide what he needed. On a number of occasions, she left the baby at home by himself for up to six hours. It was then discovered that along with the hard partying and drinking, she was addicted to acid and crystal meth. Cocaine soon followed. As a joke, people would just call her *Crystal*.

It wasn't long before a judge granted Eriq full custody of young Preston. Meanwhile, Sophia had to undergo rehabilitation at an inpatient clinic. Her success with the treatment would determine how soon she could see Preston again and possibly gain joint custody. However, neither Eriq nor his family had received word yet from the court stating such was the case. So for now, everything was fine and Preston was going nowhere.

Eriq and JaQuita sat in the café for quite a while, exchanging laughs. A few minutes turned into an hour, which then became four hours. One thing about Eriq was that he was very talkative. So, during the conversation, he spoke mostly of himself, without giving JaQuita much of a chance to talk. JaQuita, on the other hand, didn't mind because she didn't really want to reveal her true self as of yet. She just wanted to enjoy the moment. Eriq suddenly got serious.

"You don't smoke, do you?" Eriq asked.

"Ah… "

"'Cause I can't stand smokers," he replied quickly. At that instant, JaQuita remained quiet, thus causing a short pause between them.

"But you know I used to smoke," Eriq then blurted out.

"Oh, really?" asked JaQuita.

"Yeah, but I quit. You wanna know how I did it?"

"Certainly!" she exclaimed.

Eriq then began telling her his story and explaining the techniques he used to quit smoking. JaQuita listened attentively, making mental notes for herself so that she could use them to quit, which, based on his explanation, appeared very doable.

According to Eriq, he decided to do something orally that would replace his smoking habit. So he would practice taking deep breaths whenever he felt the craving, pretending he was smoking. If not that, he would gargle with salt water or disinfectants instead of smoking. And if he didn't do that, he would carry a toothbrush with him wherever he went and brush his teeth continuously whenever the desire to smoke arose. Not long after, the activities became such a routine that he forgot that he had ever smoked at all.

JaQuita was so impressed with the exercise that she knew she could do it. All that was required was making the decision to quit and taking action. She had already made up her mind to quit drinking as a result of the tragic car accident. So she knew she could also conquer her addiction to cigarettes.

"So when can I see your son? I love kids," said JaQuita.

"Well, in a couple months my little brother will be coming home to stay for the Independence Day weekend. It's not going to be big. It's just going to be the family and a few of our close relatives. It's going to be a nice cook out, too. You could come along."

"I'd love to," JaQuita replied with a smile.

Just then, Eriq looked at his watch. "Well it looks like I better get going," he said.

"Me too."

"Well, it was a pleasure meeting you JaQuita," he said.

"The pleasure was *all* mine," she remarked.

Then as the two rose up, Eriq approached JaQuita. "Listen JaQuita," he said. "I know we just met and I apologize if I seem too forward, but… when can I see you again? I mean… *before* the holiday."

JaQuita smiled, but then looked downward, appearing serious. This was the moment of truth. She was not going to pretend. That was one thing about her. She wasn't the kind to put on a façade to please other people. That would only make it worse. And according to this matter at hand, she figured this: If their relationship was meant to be, then it was *meant* to be. Simple.

"Eriq, I have something to tell you," she said.

"Go on," he replied.

"I have a felony for something I did in the past that I'm not proud of. I'm right now staying at Metrohouse until I can find a job, which I already found… I think. I don't think. In fact I'm sure. But right now I'm getting myself together and I'm really not a bad person. I just figured I'd let you know first so you don't think of me as a phony. I just hope though that you won't use my past as a means to not see me any more, because I really do want to see you… again."

Just then, Eriq's smile lit up like a Christmas tree. He admired a woman who was that up front and honest with him. "I'm gonna ask you one more time. When can I see you again?" he replied.

At that instant, JaQuita's smile rose up as well. They laughed together.

"You have to understand. We all make mistakes. I've already told you half of my story. Besides, I know a thing or two about jail. I served a few days in jail for shoplifting back in high school. Then later, I spent two weeks for a petty theft charge. My parents wanted me to stay in jail so that I would learn my lesson. And boy did I learn."

JaQuita laughed. "Can I ever come to your job to meet you, for now?" she asked.

"Certainly." He then gave her his card and pointed out his hourly schedule along with the phone number.

"Just call me a little earlier to let me know you're on your way, okay? 'Cause sometimes I can be busy training."

JaQuita nodded. "Thanks," she said.

"No problem."

Eriq then went off and within a few minutes, disappeared. Meanwhile, JaQuita couldn't help but smile throughout the entire night, just thinking about him.

6

Jackie's Miracle

THE NEXT DAY, JAQUITA PREPARED TO GO TO THE restaurant that she was supposed to have begun working at the day before. She went through the same routine to prepare, looking good and smelling fresh. She went there with pure confidence that everything was going to be fine and the owner would give her another chance.

When she got there, she asked to speak with Pacco, the owner.

"Oh I remember you. You were supposed to be here yesterday," said Georgio.

"Yeah, I know. I'm sorry, I had this thing… "

"Don't worry about it. Pacco couldn't have seen you anyway. His daughter just had a baby. A baby girl. Her name is Angela. It happened a little earlier than we expected and he was there at the hospital the whole day. It's his first grandchild. I was going to call you and tell you not to come but you didn't put down a number."

"Sorry, I... I just... "

"It's okay. You're here now."

Georgio then shifted to the other end of the counter. "Hey, yo PACCO!" he yelled.

Soon after, a short, bald overweight guy with an apron over his belly came out of the kitchen. He couldn't have been any younger than 50. "Yeah, what do ya want?" he asked.

"This lady. She's here for the waitressing job." Pacco then glanced at JaQuita for a moment.

"Congratulations on your new granddaughter," JaQuita said quickly, smiling.

Pacco then cracked a little smile, trying hard not to blush. "Oh, thank you," he answered. "You ready to work?"

JaQuita nodded in jubilation.

"Then come on to the kitchen," he gestured. "I'll give you an apron, and show you what to do. Oh and uh Georgio, don't yell my name so loud unless I won the lottery or somethin', will ya?"

"Yeah, yeah, yeah," he answered jokingly.

JaQuita then proceeded to follow Pacco to the kitchen. She was in! It would be her first job ever.

A few more weeks had passed and JaQuita had saved up the majority of her wages and tips to find a place of her own. But on this day, she was off from work and decided to take a trip to go see Peanut's mom. Since the accident, JaQuita had put off going to see the woman as a result of the entire shock. She still hadn't quite mentally grasped that it could have happened the way it did, and wanted to give some time for the mother to heal. Yet all the same, JaQuita was going to visit her just so that the mother knew that JaQuita hadn't totally forgotten about her. It was actually Peanut and her mom who took JaQuita in as a member of the family. JaQuita just hoped that the mother didn't hold any grudges against her.

When JaQuita arrived, she noticed that the house, which was a duplex, was in complete need of repair. The house needed painting and the wooden handles for the porch steps were coming apart. The sidewalk leading to the entrance was dirty and uneven. Still however, JaQuita knocked on the front door. She knocked a few more times before finally, the door opened. It was Peanut's mom.

"Hi, Miss Jacobs. It's me, JJ. Remember me?"

"Who? Oh… JJ… Jackie… is that you?"

"It's me," she nodded. JaQuita reached over and hugged her.

"I'm so sorry," JaQuita cried, clenching her hard.

"I know. I know. It's okay," she began, patting JaQuita on the back.

There was a moment of silence. "Listen, why don't you come on in?" she invited.

JaQuita did. Peanut's mom poured JaQuita a cup of coffee and the two began telling their stories. JaQuita mentioned that she had a job and was keeping her mind in a calm state. She however, never told Peanut's mother about the fight she and Peanut had before the accident. That would have been pointless.

Miss Jacobs was a recovering alcoholic herself. Though, she had been sober for nearly two years. It was her daughter, Peanut, who refused to change. Miss Jacobs was receiving social security benefits and the house her grandfather gave her a long time ago was her only possession worth writing home about. She never married. Peanut's father wasn't any better. He was currently in prison, serving seven years for multiple felonies. He never took the opportunity to visit Peanut when she was younger, and as a result, existed more as a stranger than a father.

Since then, Miss Jacobs stayed by herself with Peanut as her only reason to live. There really were no real values or goals that Miss Jacobs ever displayed. She allowed Peanut to do whatever she wanted. So therefore, anything went.

But now that Peanut was gone, nothing much went on in that house. The friends stopped coming. So it was just Miss Jacobs by herself. The only time she had company was whenever her girlfriends wanted to smoke, play cards and gossip about the latest news. JaQuita and Miss Jacobs eventually went up to the suite where Peanut once stayed. All her furniture, including her bed, couches and table set were still there along with a fridge and a stove. It was an emotional moment for both of them when they looked around.

"So when you gettin' out of Metrohouse?" Miss Jacobs asked, as she lit a cigarette.

"Well… it should be real soon. I'm expecting to meet with a landlord Friday. If I like it, I might move in right away."

Miss Jacobs wanted to respond but had a cigarette in her mouth. She then took it out rapidly, before trying to catch her breath. "Why don't you move here?" she coughed. "You don't have to buy anything major. You can use whatever you want here. What you don't want, you let me know."

"Thanks ma'am, but… I could never do that."

"Why not?"

At that moment, JaQuita was speechless. So Miss Jacobs continued. "Listen! You're already going to give your money to someone else. Right? So why not give it to me? I'll cut you a deal, anyway. You're responsible though, for your lights and gas. Besides, I'd rather rent my place to someone I know than a total stranger. Ya know what I mean? I mean I know you. And it would feel so good to have someone around that can still remind me of my baby."

At that moment, JaQuita was trapped. Miss Jacobs made an excellent point. Also, this would really help her substantially save money on furnishings, since everything was still there.

"Okay?" asked Miss Jacobs, waiting for a response.

"Okay," replied JaQuita.

"Well welcome back home," Miss Jacobs greeted as she went over to shake JaQuita's hand before hugging her again.

There was another moment of silence. JaQuita walked around the unit for a while in front of Miss Jacobs, examining the entire place before stopping at the back window. She looked downward. "Is that Peanut's other car?" she asked.

"Yeah, you want it?" asked Miss Jacobs as she blew smoke sideways.

"Well, uh… *could* I have it?"

"You sure can. Besides, my other car's back in the garage. It's the only car I've been driving anyway. It sure beats having to pay two insurance payments, I'll tell you that. You do have to fix it though. The brakes are shot, needs an oil change, and may need a new fuel pump, though I'm not sure. All I know is that she refuses to start up. I was thinking of sending it to the junk yard because I ain't going to spend that kind of money… 'specially when I got my own car."

JaQuita found it hard to sustain herself. "How much?" she asked.

"Uh… tell you what. Jus' give me 200 bucks and we'll call it a day. Besides that's more than what I would have gotten at the junk yard."

"Okay."

"Okay, then."

Miss Jacobs then thought for a moment, appearing perplexed. "Oh… I'm sorry," she said. "Where's my manners? You need a smoke? I have plenty right here."

JaQuita shook her head. "No. I don't smoke anymore. I quit."

Miss Jacobs was startled. "No shit. Really? When'd you decide to do that?"

JaQuita just shrugged her shoulders. "Something just came over me, I guess. And it just happened." At this point, JaQuita didn't feel like discussing all the details.

"Really? Wow. I'm impressed, 'cause I remember you used to smoke like a chimney when you were with us. You just couldn't wait to have a cigarette."

JaQuita didn't respond.

"*Well*... if you ever change your mind, just let me know. I got plenty," Miss Jacobs added.

JaQuita just nodded. In a nutshell, she used the techniques Eriq told her he used to quit smoking. She faltered at first, but after a month of pure effort, the cravings just vanished.

Miss Jacobs remembered one other key point she wanted to address. It was involving the condition of the house. "Before I forget, I want to make one more thing clear. There's to be no drugs in this house at all, under any circumstances. That means no cocaine. No weed. No ex. No pills. No meth—none of that. You're free to do that anywhere else but this house. And if I ever catch you doing that or bringing any of that in here, you're off my property that same night, which will be right after I call the cops. Is that clear?"

JaQuita nodded.

"I know you're on parole, but still I'm warning you. If I catch it, you're gone," Miss Jacobs stressed again.

"I understand," JaQuita replied.

"Well, all right."

JaQuita later left the house in complete disbelief over the recent chain of events. She could hardly stay still. It was a fatal car crash that catapulted all these results in her life. And if that was the case, Eriq just *had* to be the one for her. The two of them, by the way, started seeing each other regularly.

The next day, JaQuita couldn't wait to tell Mandi her story. She probably would have flipped out of her chair. Based on the fact that JaQuita's urine was always clean, she only had to see Mandi once a month now. However, the two still kept in contact. They were developing a solid bond. Mandi enjoyed JaQuita just as JaQuita enjoyed Mandi. It was usually not ethical to invite clients into one's personal life, but suddenly Mandi believed she could trust JaQuita, and wanted to invite her to Riley's birthday party, which was going to be in a couple weeks. By this time, JaQuita was now on her sixth book that Mandi had given her to read.

"I met someone!" JaQuita exclaimed. "Well actually, he met me. And it was just like you said… things come into your life when you least expect it."

"Yes indeed," replied Mandi with joy. "So who is he?"

"His name's Eriq. He's a fitness trainer at a gym that's not too far from here. He's real handsome too. You should see this guy. I mean… *man*! I mean this brotha is as fine as May wine. Ya *feel* me?"

"I heard that."

"Plus, he comes from a Church family. They're Baptists. His mom directs the choir and he has a brother that goes to college. But Eriq has a son, though. He's so adorable. He's smart too. We have such an amazing time. I've seen him a number of times already. His name's Preston. He's five."

"And the girl?" Mandi inquired.

"Oh… she's in treatment some place. She lost custody of him. She's just a crack ho… so… you know, it's not like she can get Eriq back or anything."

Mandi burst out laughing. "Wow! Well I am so proud of you!"

JaQuita then looked at Mandi for a moment, squarely in the eye. "I wish you had been my mom. The reason all these things are happening is because of you. You changed my whole life. You made me discover how sweet it is to be alive."

"Oh now JaQuita. Don't make me start crying," Mandi said as she began moving her arms around, trying to conceal her face.

Mandi changed the subject. "So what about your job?" she asked.

"I got it. I'm a waitress now. And let me tell you somethin', it was that sort of feeling you kept telling me about that prompted me to go in there. And it was so strange... because I sort of felt that I knew I already got the job before they said it themselves."

"All right! I'm happy for you. How 'bout a place to stay? Have you found one yet?"

"Yup, and I got to tell you about that too. Ya know that accident that happened a while back? Well I knew a few of the passengers in that car. And I went to go see the mom who later said I could live in the top unit since no one was there anymore."

"Wow."

"Yeah, and I already have all the furniture, refrigerator, stove and kitchen table set that was already in there. The only thing I had to bring was my clothes. That's it."

"Alleluia. Praise the Lord. Tell me more."

"I also got a car too, which was the spare car of the woman's daughter. She ended up givin' it to me for only $200. The only work I needed to do was change the fuel pump, put on new brakes, and change the oil. She must've thought it was a lot of money, but to me, it wasn't."

"Amen to that. What kind of car is it?"

"A Toyota."

Now at that moment, Mandi was in shock. She remembered that same brand being in the first picture taped to the goal book she gave JaQuita. Any and everything was coming into full bloom. All of this occurred in just a few months? Even Mandi underestimated the speed in which dreams could travel through thought.

There once lived a man by the name of Napoleon Hill, who was considered by many to be one of the greatest, if not *the* greatest motivational genius of all time. He was the author of *The Law of Success in 16 Lessons* and *Think and Grow Rich*. He was once given the assignment to observe and study the most powerful and wealthiest people of his time, so as to determine the common elements that made them all successful. After conducting his investigation, he was to then gather the data and document it in a book form as an inspiration for mankind.

The men he interviewed were Andrew Carnegie, Henry Ford, John D. Rockefeller, Franklin D. Roosevelt, Thomas Edison, and many others. The assignment was actually awarded to him by Andrew Carnegie, who was the owner of U.S. Steel and considered the richest man on earth around the year 1908. The purpose of the project was to give the average man the opportunity to develop himself in whichever direction he chose through thought and the law of attraction. The entire mission took 20 years to complete.

Napoleon made some startling discoveries during the research and was dazzled by how simple the law of attraction worked, yet was even more surprised that not many people knew of its existence or how to apply it correctly. The elite at that time knew of its power, and as a group, campaigned never to reveal the secret to the masses. It was not to ever be taught in schools or appear in magazines, news articles, or even books. To keep their power, they wanted to keep the masses ignorant of this great law. This would then explain part of the reason of why the rich were getting richer and the poor were getting poorer.

It was even alleged that Henry Ford played a huge role in preventing such knowledge from ever reaching the public. It's been said that he once told his peers: *"If we release this information, who will work in my factories?"*

In the early 1900s, Napoleon appeared before Congress at the Washington, D.C. Chamber of Commerce to discuss the law of attraction. During the conference, he said this: " …the law of attraction, when applied, is so effective and so powerful, and works 100% of the time, that it frightens me."

True story.

So one could imagine the look on Mandi's face when JaQuita began telling her all the manifestations that were occurring in her life within such a short time. Yes, the law of attraction was that effective and worked that quickly. All a person needed was the right attitude, belief, and it shall be done.

"Well, now you know it works. I don't have to tell you anything else," said Mandi.

"Of course you can," JaQuita replied. "There's still so much to learn."

Mandi then caught herself. "You know I never imagined you were this intelligent. Of course there is. It's a process that takes a few minutes to learn but a lifetime to master. And you already know that. You do have a humble spirit. I now also wish you were my child." JaQuita smiled. "But since you brought it up, I want to tell you something," Mandi continued.

"What's that?"

"Well, from everything you said, it's important to know that as long as you're feeling joy and happiness consistently, there will never be any bad things that will plague you. Some things may initially appear as a bad thing, but they are only situations that are designed to ultimately work in your favor. Basically, the universe uses events that may appear to the world as bad, but determines it to be the best way to suit your interests."

"Such as… ?" inquired JaQuita.

"I'll give you an example. When I was in high school, I was in love with this guy. His name was Fletcher Campbell. I loved that boy so much that I thought the two of us would be in love forever. I thought that after college, we would get married, have kids, and live happily ever after. That was my dream. And I was so happy all the time just thinking about it. Well one day, I went into his house since it was never a problem before, and found him in bed on top of my best friend. Her name was Judi Hall. As soon as I found out, I instantly ran away crying, feeling so devastated, so depressed. I almost thought that no man was any good or trustworthy. Well, wouldn't you know that 20 years later, my sister Carla called me up to tell me that Fletcher was in jail and was looking at facing 10 years for assault and almost beating a woman to death. It turned out that he had a list of felonies and prior cases, causing him to go in and out of jail since high school."

JaQuita was in shock. "Are you serious?" she asked.

"Yeah. I later went by to visit him in prison to confirm the story and he did admit to beating that woman, who was at the time in intensive care. But what was so surprising, was that I already had a secret intent on sharing the law of attraction with someone which I never told him about. Yet during our conversation, he suggested on his own for me to become a parole officer due to the number of inmates who he felt could be inspired by me based on how he saw me develop into the person I now was. And it was right there that I actually felt spirit talking to me through him that I later took his advice and became a parole officer. And... *here* I am. The rest is history."

"So you finding out he was with someone else... sort of... *saved* your life?"

"I want to say so. Now it's a possibility that I may have left once I discovered he was getting too violent. However, who knows if I would have left in time. Maybe I may not have had the chance."

"Sure you're right. I can definitely relate with that," JaQuita responded. "And if it wasn't for him suggesting that to you, I may have never found you."

"*Maybe.*"

"And who knows where I would have been by then," added JaQuita.

"You're right. Who knows?"

"So let's recap your situation," said Mandi. "Do you feel that the car crash of your friends, though tragic, helped you obtain your goals?"

"I know it did, because it was the news of the crash that led me to miss my bus stop that brought me to Eriq, while I was trying to get to my new job, which wasn't even necessary to attend, since the manager wasn't there due to the fact that *he* was awaiting the birth of his new granddaughter. And it was that car crash that led me to get the house I needed to move into, which later got me a car at a cheap price. *Plus*, in between there, I was able to quit smoking and drinking."

Out of excitement, JaQuita paused for a moment before eventually calming down to address something less exciting, which pertained to the car accident. "Yet still, I don't want my fortune to be someone else's *mis*fortune," she said.

"You can never give someone else misfortune by having fortune yourself," Mandi replied. "That's a misconception. Your friends attracted their own misfortune. Staying positive did save your life, but did not harm them in any way, shape or form. Had you gotten in that car, there would have been six deaths instead of five."

There was a moment of silence while each woman pondered the story. "*So*… there you have it," Mandi then added. "It's the universe sending out a signal in the best way it can based on its own projections, to provide you in the best way possible to receive that which you want. So my message to you is: never ever look at any situation as being bad. Just take it as a challenge that will eventually turn out to your advantage. You may *think* you know what's right for you, but trust me, the universe knows best, since it's aware of every variable in its existence. As long as you just stress the *feeling* or intention of what you want, the universe will find the proper means of giving it to you, so that you have that same feeling, which sometimes, may cause you a little *pain* in the process. As for me, I wanted a good and loving husband, and so it granted me Ronnie, even though I *thought* it was Fletcher all along. Almost 100% of every event that will ever occur in your life are things you can never see with your own two eyes. So just relax and let the universe take control. Believe me, its got you covered."

JaQuita was amazed to hear this, but rather than dwell on that situation, she slightly changed the subject for the sake of time. "Can I ask you a question?"

"Sure. Anything."

"How do you know if a man is *the* one? I mean, this is my first real relationship and everything is goin' on fine, but… how do you know? Like how did *you* finally know? I mean my guess is that you were already married before you later found out about Fletcher."

Mandi nodded, pausing for a moment, before speaking. "Well… that's a subject you can't fully explain, JaQuita. I guess… you just know, you know? I mean when the feeling is right, you'll know. All I can say is make sure he knows how you feel and find out his reaction. That will tell you. I remember when I first asked Fletcher if he loved me, he began to stutter and sort of look sideways, but replied 'yes' anyway. That was a red flag which I failed to realize at that time because again, I was in love with him. But just remember this, eyes never lie."

"Well I'm thinking about poppin' the big question."

"JaQuita, c'mon. So soon? Naw."

"I jus' said I was thinking about it. I didn't say I'd do it."

"Well good. Make sure you think it through, though. Okay? Because… marriage is a *big* step. Trust me. I know."

"Okay." There was another moment of pause. "I have just one more question," JaQuita said.

"This really has been bugging me for a while. I understand earlier what you said when we first met, about you helping former inmates and things like that, but honestly Mandi, why did you decide to devote your time teaching me this secret? I mean what's the real reason? Don't get me wrong. I will be forever grateful to you, but… *why*?"

Mandi thought real hard in deciding whether this was the right time to tell her story. The time it was going to take her didn't matter, since JaQuita was supposedly her last client before lunch. So even if the conversation ran into her break, she didn't mind. She enjoyed JaQuita's company. Therefore, she decided to reveal.

"You got time?" she asked.

"*Yeah*. I mean, why me?"

"Well… it was a promise I made to a very dear friend of mine a long time ago. She had helped me and asked that I share the material with someone else."

"Which friend? I mean what was her name?"

"Her name… was Francine. Francine Williamson. I shall never forget her for as long as I live. She saved *my* life. If it wasn't for her, I wouldn't be here today."

"How?"

Just then, a knock appeared at the door. "Come in," Mandi replied.

A young white man entered the room, appearing to be Mandi's co-worker on the same floor. He wore a tie and a work badge around his neck. "Remember we have that meeting in about fifteen minutes," he said.

Mandi had totally forgotten. The meeting completely slipped her mind. "Oh yes. Thanks Chris," she said. "I'll be there right away."

He then said "okay" and left, closing the door behind him.

"Well I have to go, Jackie. Listen, we'll continue this discussion next month. All right?"

"Yes ma'am."

"Oh and before I forget, continue to still write your dreams down and post pictures. Don't stop. You got to constantly build and be hungry. Don't just stay still and relax. Continue expanding, okay? It's a road that never ends. Think of your mind as a flower. Either it's growing, or it's dying, but it can never stay still."

"Got it," JaQuita answered.

Mandi then smiled. "You know, I'm very proud of you JaQuita. Honestly I am. Success begins with a decision and you've shown that. You are the first person I met thus far who has actually been coachable and willing to change. You never did complain or argue with me. You are the perfect apprentice. And for that, I salute you. I already know you'll do fine and go far in life with this. And I now know, in my heart of hearts, that my place here on this planet mattered. Now c'mon, give me a hug before I'm late for my meeting."

They then hugged each other tight as if for the last time.

"I love you," said JaQuita.

"I love you too."

Then after a few minutes, JaQuita was gone.

"Good luck to you child," Mandi whispered to herself. "Good luck."

7

⋙⋘

Meet the Family

JaQuita was so excited to be attending Eriq's family get-together. She couldn't wait to see his family. To Eriq, JaQuita was a true warrior. To experience all that she went through, and then continue strong with a positive mindset, was something he admired and appreciated about her. It was that which made him swear to himself to never lay his hand on her for as long as he lived. He was raised to respect women anyway. His father never struck his mother.

JaQuita was lucky. Her job gave her the holiday off. So, Eriq picked her up that day from her new house. She was stunning. Her hair was micro braided and held back in a nice pony tail. She had on light cherry-colored lipstick. She wore sky-blue jeans with razor-sharp creases down the middle. On top was a simple white dress shirt that was tucked in, with her beautiful smile to go along with it, not to mention her perfume, which had a nice rose scent. She also wore new white Adidas tennis shoes with a blue logo. So yes, it would appear that she was ready to go.

Her physique was perfect. At 5'5" and 135 pounds, she had a wonderful body. What was most appealing was her rear. It was nice and firm, enough to make any guy stare. Plus, she had full breasts. She almost looked like a model. But in spite of these sexy features, she still always dressed in good taste, which made her even more attractive in Eriq's mind.

Eriq didn't have to honk the horn, because JaQuita was right in front of the porch, waiting. Her car was now fixed, however, she wanted Eriq to retrain her on how to drive. She had learned how in the past, but since her release from prison, she wanted to just hone her skills a little more before she was back on the road.

"Baby, you look gorgeous."

"Thank you," she said. "You're not bad yourself."

She then kissed his cheek as she entered the car. Eriq had on a tight t-shirt that showed the definition of his chest and muscles. He always liked to show off. And he wore jeans. Young Preston was in the back in his own little world, playing with his toys, but greeted JaQuita when she got into the car. They were going to Eriq's parents' house, which was in a suburb a few miles west of Detroit.

When they arrived, there didn't appear to be that many people there. Eriq directed JaQuita to the backyard where he introduced her to his parents.

"Well hi. I'm Martha, Eriq's mother. How are you doin'?"

"Just fine Mrs. Buher. And you?"

"The same… ooooh, and you're formal too. My son must've picked him a good one here," she said jokingly. "You're very pretty."

"Thank you," JaQuita replied.

"You're welcome and this here is my husband. His name's Ernie."

"How do ya do?" he greeted, shaking her hand.

"Fine, sir."

Ernie then hobbled off using a cane as a result of his job injury years ago.

Martha continued. "And finally, this is my other son, Justin. I don't know if Eriq told you but he goes to Michigan State."

"Yes he told me. You're a *Spartan*," she joked at him.

Justin laughed. He was a bit dazzled by her charm. He knew his brother had a weakness in choosing good women, but at first glance, he sensed that maybe, this one could be a different story. Justin was also well built, but not as athletic as his brother. He was more talented on the scholastic side.

Martha then began introducing JaQuita to a few of the other family members, a brother-in-law and two sisters. There were only four other couples at the party, so fortunately, it wasn't too drawn out. The entire event was fun. JaQuita was laughing, having a good time and playing mostly with Preston. Eriq was studying her from afar and sensed a good spirit about her. He almost didn't believe what she told him about her past. He just couldn't sense any pain in her. But he didn't want to find out, either. Who she was now was fine by him.

At the picnic, there was music, ribs, hot dogs, hamburgers, macaroni and cheese, collard greens, peach cobbler, sweet potato pie, and rice—just the usual soul food. There were games such as flag football, which was played at a nearby park, along with volleyball, which JaQuita participated in. In all, everyone had a blast.

Once it was over, everyone else left while Eriq's family stayed behind. They were too tired to clean up. All that was done was the packing of the trash in a huge dumpster. The dishes and the food just stayed on the kitchen counter and in the sink. All the crumbs and little items on the floor could stay until tomorrow. The family, along with JaQuita, were circled around a big table outside, just sitting down, exhausted. For some reason, JaQuita was silent staring downward to the table, while her right foot kept tapping rapidly against the pavement. It was a noise everyone could hear. Eriq was sitting right across from her. Justin was beside her with Martha on the other side. Preston sat beside his father while Ernie, Eriq's father, was sitting between Preston and Martha.

"So did you enjoy yourself today?" asked Martha.

JaQuita wasn't paying attention. It was like she was in her own little world. So Martha asked her again, shoving her by the shoulder to get her attention.

"Huh… oh, sorry. Yes. I enjoyed myself very much. Thank you."

"Yeah, I saw you out there havin' fun," Martha added.

JaQuita didn't respond. She continued making that tapping noise with her feet which suddenly started to get annoying.

"Is something the matter honey?" asked Martha again. "You seem to not be with us. It's like you're no longer a part of this planet."

That was because JaQuita was in heavy thought right now. And she always tapped her foot when she was in deep thought. Ironically, this always occurred before she was about to say something big. And she was debating whether to say it now or wait. *Go by your feelings*, was the message Mandi always told her, which kept resonating through JaQuita's mind. She was also reminded to remove fear and remain self confident by saying what was on her mind, as discussed in the book *The Magic of Thinking Big*. So, without further delay, she decided to just go out and say what was on her mind. To hell with the consequences. Like she once said, she didn't want to be seen as a phony.

Without answering Martha's question, JaQuita looked directly at Eriq. "Eriq, I want to say something I feel you should know. Now, my background isn't that clean. I know that. I never went to college. I know that too. And we've only gone together for only a few months now. Now I might not be the smartest or brightest person in the world, but of all the things that I do know, I know this for sure: I love you. The great energy that I feel when I'm with you and your family can only make sense if there is a similar connection we all share together. It's genuine. It's strong, and boy is it real. It's a feeling I haven't felt in so long and I don't ever want it to go away. And I would feel no greater joy right now than if you made me your wife... Mrs. Buher."

After she had finished, she looked back down at the table. There was utter silence. It was so quiet that if a person took his time, he could hear the heartbeat of an ant. No one said anything for several minutes. Everyone was just in complete shock, as if the feds suddenly stormed into the house unannounced before saying to them, 'wrong house'. Eriq was short of words himself; completely off guard. If this were baseball, JaQuita just pitched to him a nasty fastball hot enough to go 102 miles an hour. He just never saw that coming. Yet it was evident, he had to say something. Though still, it was like his tongue was paralyzed. Where would he start?

Finally, Martha got completely tired of the suspense and jumped in. "Well? Say something. The girl *is* talking to you," she told him, kicking his feet.

"Well... I-I-I don't... know w-what to say... "

"Just say 'yes,'" JaQuita answered quickly. "I mean... if you... really want to."

"But right now, we... don't have... I mean how... "

"The *how*," she interrupted. "The *how* is not important. It's irrelevant. In fact, don't even worry about the *how*. Everything will take care of itself. Believe me."

For a moment, Eriq felt like JaQuita had some form dementia. But in truth, he just didn't know what JaQuita knew. He was confused.

"Oh? So what makes you such an expert?" he asked.

"If you marry me, I'll tell you. Besides, it's part of how we met in the first place."

Eriq stood silent. Suddenly Preston got involved. "Marry her, Daddy," he said. "She's cool."

Eriq looked closely at the boy and could see the excitement in his eyes, which brought such a warm feeling to Eriq's heart. Just hearing those words from his son meant an awful lot.

"Why are you making it so complicated son?" Ernie then added.

"Is there someone else?" Martha asked.

"Hell no!" Eriq responded sharply, feeling a bit insulted by the question.

"Well then what's the problem?"

Eriq didn't answer.

Martha then shifted to JaQuita, smiling. "You have to forgive him, sweetheart," Martha explained. "At times he can be a little stubborn. He's always been that way ever since he was a little boy. But I don't know why he's acting this way now. He's always wanted a woman that's outspoken. I don't know his problem."

"So what's it gonna be brotha?" Justin began asking, also getting involved. He was smiling too, which annoyed Eriq. He knew perfectly well that Justin loved putting him on the spot during moments like this. They'd always fight over that throughout their childhood years.

"What, you think this is funny? Just remember, we may be grown now, but I can still kick yo ass," Eriq replied.

At that moment, Preston instantly put his hands over his ears.

"Well then come on with it," Justin replied. "Just remember though, it's you with the situation. Not me."

Just then, Eriq got up from his chair, appearing to want to take Justin on, which was more than likely just a show to impress JaQuita.

"Okay guys, guys. Fellas. *Children!*" Martha intervened. "It's really not that deep. Now it's obvious that Eriq and JaQuita need some time alone. So what we're going to do is get outta here and catch that huge sale they got over there at Benny's."

"But grandma, you said that's… "

"*Tonight!* The sale is tonight. They just changed it," she snapped, alerting Preston to keep quiet. "And we have to go… NOW… before they close."

Just then, JaQuita began giggling. She just couldn't help herself. She was going to enjoy this family.

Everyone then proceeded to leave the table except for her and Eriq. Within minutes everyone was ready to go to the store. While this was going on, however, Martha began unhooking all the phone lines from the walls before putting them in her purse. She had a habit of overdoing things at times.

When Eriq saw this, he went over to her. "Ma. What'ch ya doin'?"

"Listen! This is probably the most important decision you will ever make in your lifetime. You hear me? And keep in mind, your boy Preston, *needs* a mother. So I don't want any phone calls or call devices that will distract your attention. I want you to focus and answer that girl. You got it?"

Eriq tried to calm her down, but Martha resisted. "Don't you start with me," she warned. "Now everyone's at the car and I got to go. So… just go back there and leave me alone."

Eriq had no recourse. His mom had won, as usual. What was interesting was that JaQuita was still at the table, laughing, overhearing the whole conversation.

"Oh and by the way," Martha shouted, ensuring JaQuita could also hear her. "You all take all the time you need! We're going to be gone for a very loooong time. You hear me? Byyyye now!"

At that instant, the door slammed and Martha was gone. Eriq had no other choice but to head back to JaQuita. He then sat down in the chair across from her. Slowly the two raised their heads simultaneously before looking each other straight in the eyes. Then suddenly, they began laughing loudly. It took a while for them both to catch their breaths.

Once they were done, Eriq then reached out to grab her right hand. But rather than submit, JaQuita went around the table over to him. He then took that same hand, held it gently in both his hands and kissed it softly before whispering, "*Yes.*" He then rose up and the two began hugging and kissing.

"I love you," she cried.

"Me too." Eriq held her face, looked her into her eyes and kissed her forehead before placing her head to his chest. It was then JaQuita sensed the sincerity in his heart.

A moment of silence followed. Then after a few minutes, Eriq said something. "You know, my mom *did* say that they were going to be gone for a very long time. So… what's up?"

JaQuita lifted her chin up at Eriq before quickly looking back down with a smile. "How long?" she wondered.

"Long enough. Trust me. I know." JaQuita laughed with Eriq and later that night, the two of them made love in the guest room. It was an exciting moment for each of them. Though after an hour had passed, Eriq suddenly realized that they were still in his parents' house. So he rushed to quickly take JaQuita home.

When they got there, JaQuita smiled, waving to him as she left the car. Eriq waved back but continued to stare at her as she went to the porch. JaQuita then turned around as she opened the door, noticing that Eriq had suddenly turned off his engine. Seconds later, he came out of the car and went towards her at the front porch. JaQuita, a little excited, began smiling even more as he came up.

"Could I just make myself a quick cup of coffee?" he asked. "I promise I won't be long. It's just so I can be alert to do my routine workout once I get back home."

Immediately, JaQuita began laughing, and Eriq smiled. Without saying a word, JaQuita just glanced at him before finally turning around to walk upstairs to her place.

"Just lock the door behind you," she told him.

Eriq did just that and followed her. Once upstairs, he immediately rushed behind JaQuita by surprise and carried her to the bedroom where they made love again the entire night.

A few hours later, around 2 a.m., JaQuita rested against Eriq's shoulder, softly rubbing his chest and biceps as his right arm wrapped around her body.

"Baby?" she eventually uttered.

"Yes?"

"What ever happened to that cup of coffee?"

Eriq looked at her. "Oh... I'm sorry," he said. "I thought *you* were the coffee. After all, your skin looks just like it."

JaQuita couldn't help laughing, and neither could Eriq. One thing was certain. Eriq definitely knew how to make her laugh.

8

❧❧

Mrs. Buher

JaQuita could not wait to tell Mandi the good news. Eriq had already bought her a gold ring with a small stone in the middle, which she wore on her left finger as an engagement ring. She would show it off wherever she went. Whether it was at work, at home, or outside—she was just so happy. She wanted to have at least five children. Since she was by herself without family members, she figured, why not have the company to account for the space? Eriq was not too keen on the idea, but JaQuita would always answer back, saying, "we'll see." She also wrote it down in her goal book.

Sex was an absolute must in the relationship, and occurred at least twice a week. Anytime JaQuita called to tell Eriq, "coffee's ready," he knew *exactly* what time it was. "I'll be right there," he'd say.

It was incredible, too. According to JaQuita, Eriq was "the man." However, she didn't want to get pregnant until she was officially married, so she used birth control pills. She didn't mind condoms, but the pleasure was more intense and sat-isfying without one; and since neither of them had a disease, Eriq never wore them. And he had no problem with that.

JaQuita also decided to change her name officially to "Jackie." For some reason, she just wasn't fond of "JaQuita." So later that week, she went to the social security office and officially changed her name. It was now "Jackie Jenkins." She then used the document to change her ID and all of her other personal records. Eriq was pleased with the change. Though he didn't care one way or the other, "Jackie" sure had a more familiar appeal. To Jackie, the name itself gave her a new identity as a symbol of a new lady of old.

A week had passed and it was now time to see Mandi again. Jackie was so eager to see her that she came an hour before the appointment, having the notion that Mandi might see her a little earlier and that maybe, they could have a lit-tle bit more time to talk. Since Mandi was already married, maybe she could give Jackie advice on what dress to wear, what style to make her hair, or what hall to rent out. All these ideas kept running through Jackie's head and she knew she and Mandi were going to have so much fun talking about them.

When she got there, she walked over to the desk to sign in, but she could not find her name on the sheet under Mandi Harris's docket. Her name wasn't listed with any of the parole officers. So Jackie went over to the window to find out what was wrong. An older lady was on the phone when she ar-rived. Jackie waited until she was done with the call.

"Yes?" the attendant asked.

"Yes. My name's Jackie and I have an appointment with Mandi Harris. Is she in?"

"Let me check. Just one moment," she said.

She went to the computer. Then looked into the file cabi-net to check some records before making a call to someone who seemed to be her manager. Then she slammed down the phone. "She's no longer employed here," she said.

Jackie was surprised. No. There had to be a mistake. And even if Mandi left, she wouldn't do so without saying good-bye at least. Would she? Both she and Jackie had grown so close.

"What? Are you sure? Please check again," Jackie demanded.

"I did check again. You saw all that work I was doing and I confirmed it with our head office. She's gone."

Jackie's heart sank. She didn't know how to react. She had all this good news to share and now was confused. Just then, the woman told her to sit in a chair because the manager wanted to see her.

A few minutes passed and a tall stocky man approached her. "Are you JaQuita?" he asked.

"It's Jackie, now… but yeah, that's me."

"Okay my name is Frank. Could you come with me to the office, please?"

"Sure," she replied. Jackie followed the man to his office.

"You can have a seat if you want," he said. Jackie sat down. "Listen, I'm going to get straight to the point. Mandi's no longer here. Without getting into specifics, it's said that she conducted practices within the department that were considered inappropriate and unethical. Now the details are irrelevant and I'm not really concerned of your relations with her. But what I want to do is give you something that she asked me to give you."

He then reached under his desk and pulled out three shoe boxes that were each wrapped in a brown paper bag with duck tape around them that read: *To JaQuita Jenkins*.

The man handed them to Jackie. She tried shaking them to guess what they might be, but there seemed to be no movement or sound. Whatever was inside seemed to be able to fit in each box from one end to the other without providing any space whatsoever for noise.

"So... who's my new parole officer?" Jackie asked.

Frank leaned against his chair with the back of his head in the palms of his hands.

"There is no parole officer for you anymore," he said.

"What?" she asked.

"Well, it seems here that the department issued you an early release since you've never had tainted urine all this while and attended all your meetings regularly. Plus, you've never been in trouble with the law. So they thought it was just a waste of time bringing you in here any longer especially since our caseloads are so full of people that do belong here. So... you're free to go. I just need your signature here on this paper which confirms that fact."

Frank then released the paper and placed it on the desk, giving Jackie a pen to use. Jackie glanced at the paper for a moment before signing. Frank then took the sheet.

"Thank *you*," he said, before giving Jackie her copy.

Jackie took it before looking at him once more. "So... so what now?" she asked.

Frank looked at her strangely. "You can leave now," he said. "If not that, at least stay in the lobby—just not in my office. My only advice to you is: stay outta trouble and... good luck."

Jackie left, feeling a bit relieved but upset. Her parole was supposed to be a year, but she only served seven months and was now free. And while that was great, she felt a little betrayed by the whole matter. She thought if anything, Mandi would at least have notified her somehow or communicated with her so they could still develop their close bond. She had respected Mandi as her mentor; her friend; her savior. Who else now was going to understand Jackie or be that inspirational?

As it turned out, Mandi had been under massive pressure for several months by the administration she worked for.

Unlike other parole officers who only conducted the standard routine of asking their clients how they were doing and encouraging them not to get into trouble, Mandi took her job a step further. She tried empowering her clients by giving them books to read and teaching them about the law of attraction. Nothing ever indicated, however, that she wasn't doing her job, but the positive nature she displayed made the co-workers around her jealous, as it seemed to make them look bad.

News of this was always brought to the attention of the head of the department. And in these meetings, Mandi admitted to such actions but adamantly stated that she was doing nothing wrong, and that sharing the books and information would give the former inmates something productive to work towards rather than doing something that could land them back in prison.

Though the truth behind the matter was, that the system desired that these same inmates go back to prison, since it was the fuel for which the department stayed funded, which in turn, maintained the jobs for all its managers and parole officers. Therefore, there really was no benefit empowering them. The burden was put on the ex-convicts to figure out their own way to stay out of trouble.

But in order to conceal its true agenda, the department stated that Mandi's actions weren't part of the mandate and that she should cease from such activities or be forced to resign.

When she refused, she was met with heavy opposition from the administrative director, who then demanded that her entire desk be cleared and that she no longer have access to her clients. Even though this type of action was unlawful, the director threatened to bring false allegations against her that could eventually destroy her career, her reputation, and the lives of her family. And that wasn't a battle Mandi was willing to take on. So, she left quietly.

When this happened, all she could think about was Jackie, her favorite student. However, during this time, Jackie had already moved from *Metrohouse*, and her new phone was not yet on for Mandi to call her. And Jackie had not yet given Mandi her new address, and didn't know where Mandi lived. The assumption was that Mandi would still be employed by the parole office, and that Jackie could call her at work if she needed to. Therefore, neither party had exchanged personal information, since there was never any anticipation of this ever happening.

So, with no other way to communicate, Mandi packed a bunch of books into three shoe boxes for Jackie, along with a letter, which she pleaded with one of the workers to give to her. They were all books that handled the elements needed to develop a better character and possess more power in manifesting dreams into realities. They were books Mandi had read through the years that had a massive effect on her personal life and development. Almost half of the books contained in those boxes were already read by Jackie. So now she had something to always refer back to.

As Jackie went down the steps outside the building, she found a high platform and sat down to open the boxes. She glanced at all the books Mandi gave her to read. They were:

Title	Author
The Magic of Thinking Big	David J. Schwartz
How to Win Friends and Influence People	Dale Carnegie
The Power of Positive Thinking	Norman Vincent Peale
The Greatest Salesman in the World	Og Mandino
See You at the Top	Zig Ziglar
Hung By the Tongue	Francis P. Martin
What You Say is What You Get	Don Gossett
As a Man Thinketh	James Allen
The Magic of Believing	Claude M. Bristol
The Science of Getting Rich	Wallace D. Wattles
Think and Grow Rich	Napoleon Hill
The Law of Success in Sixteen Lessons	Napoleon Hill

How to Have Confidence and Power in Dealing with People	*Les Giblin*
Psycho-cybernetics	*Maxwell Maltz*
How I Raised Myself from Failure to Success in Selling	*Frank Bettger*

In between two of the books was an envelope addressed to her that read, *JaQuita Jenkins*, on the front. It was sealed. Jackie placed the shoe boxes beside her and opened the letter.

Dear JaQuita,

You probably know by now that I no longer work at the office. It was suggested that I leave the administration. By you having been in the legal system and understanding how it works, I'm sure you can determine on your own what happened. Anyway, when this happened, all I could think of was you and the wonderful relationship we shared. I truly missed our conversations and how we inspired each other. You were truly my best student and a blessing in my life. I am so grateful to have known you. Just seeing you, gives me joy and makes me believe that there are still a lot of good folks out there despite their past history. All they need is to be educated on the positive way of thinking so that they too can receive blessings. Along with this letter, are books which I'm passing on to you. I have read all of them and have all the copies which I still read to this day. They have been treasures that have inspired me, inspired my family, and created so many blessings in our lives, and have changed us for the better as human beings. Everything I know and teach is in these books. These books will give you inspiration, power, and above all, the will to believe that you can achieve whatever it is that you want.

My only prayer is that you will read and reread them as often as possible and use them wisely for the betterment of yourself and others around you. Don't ever stop dreaming. Keep believing and understand that God made you right. He made you great and He made you powerful.

Don't ever forget that, and always remember to model that same character in everything you do. I trust you will go far and believe that one day we will see each other again someday and tell our stories. I love you and wish you the very best in life. May The Heavenly Father continue to always shine in your life and as I have passed this onto you, so I ask that you pass this onto someone else.

Enormous blessings will come your way. Trust me. There's more than enough love to go around in this lifetime. I bid you farewell and ask that you take care of yourself. Respect yourself. Love yourself, and be yourself. But above all, always dare to dream BIG! You are a limitless creation.

Love always,

Mandi Harris

PS: I want to leave you with this quote and wish that you remember it always.

"Whatever the mind of man can conceive and bring itself to believe, it can achieve."
—*Napoleon Hill*

Jackie broke down in tears. She was very touched by the letter and the gifts. Mandi gave her something that even gold could not buy. Of course anyone can buy the books. However it was the power that these books trigger in the mind that was well beyond what a million Rockefellers could buy. Books create ideas and ideas are bulletproof. In other words, once created, ideas are indestructible. And that was primarily Mandi's message to Jackie.

Dr. Martin Luther King Jr. and Abraham Lincoln for example, may have been murdered, but what couldn't be murdered were their ideas. And it's their ideas that have spread throughout the globe, continuing to inspire people who weren't even born when these men were alive. Currencies, holidays, streets, schools, institutions, playgrounds, monuments, foundations, and many other areas have all been named in their honor. That's what ideas do. They inspire and last forever.

Since everything is energy, books themselves carry a vibration, which in effect, causes the mind to imagine once the words are being read. And from these imaginations come ideas. And isn't it amazing that Dr. Martin Luther King Jr. and Abraham Lincoln were both avid readers, which in effect, helped them create their ideas?

As a result, this would explain why there's so much emphasis on game shows, sitcoms, soap operas, and other forms of entertainment that stress very little, if any, importance on reading. Is it any wonder why an increasing number of people of all ages in the United States— considered the richest land on earth—have grown to be illiterate despite the fact they've all been to *school*?

Any observant person can easily realize that the entire process is instinctively crafted by design. Why? Because the powers that be know the power of reading, which is why entertainment has been such a valuable tool in distracting the human mind. Thinkers promote fear to the "establishment."

Another way of putting it comes from a phrase heard in various ways by different people: "If you want to ever hide anything valuable or important, put it in a book."

Og Mandino, who was a world renowned author of many books, particularly *The Greatest Salesman in the World,* which was an instant classic, was at a convention speaking in front of a large crowd of people. And in one of his speeches, he quoted another motivational speaker named Charlie "Tremendous" Jones. And in that speech, what Charlie said, according to Og, was this: "You will be the same person in five years as you are today, except for the people you meet and the books you read."

Books are power. And what Mandi gave Jackie, was *power!* And since Jackie had seen results already, she just had to continue on course with her feelings, thoughts and reading. However, it was important for Jackie to expand more upon her goals. No goal was too big or too small for the universe to create in her life. And one of the goals she later put down in her dream book was to see Mandi again. Beside that message were several stars she drew to symbolize the need. While the gift of the power to control her own destiny was such an extraordinary blessing, the most precious gift Mandi gave to Jackie was love, unconditional love.

As far as Eriq and Jackie were concerned, their relationship was still solid. They continued spending time with each other. Whenever they were both free, they'd take walks in a park or go to a movie holding hands. Sometimes Eriq would give Jackie driving lessons, but the instructions were inconsistent due to Eriq's job. So what should have probably taken a week or two to learn, ended up taking two months. In the end though, Jackie eventually got the hang of it and was later awarded her driver's license. She was now on the road.

Jackie had grown to be very fond of young Preston. Occasionally, she would take him to an open field to fly his kite and buy him ice cream. One time, she even tried teaching him how to ride a bike. She was real happy he was in her life, because it gave her practice for when she and Eriq would have children together.

She also made it a point to develop a good relationship with Eriq's parents. Both Jackie and Martha spent quality time together, learning about each other. They had a few differences from time to time, but none too serious. For the most part, Martha liked Jackie and felt she would make a decent wife, which was far more than she could say about the past women in Eriq's life. Since Jackie hadn't much experience in cooking, Martha was more than happy to help her learn, since Eriq loved to eat. Eventually, Jackie began making simple meals that later became favorites of Eriq and his family.

As time progressed however, Jackie began getting irritated that there was no date set yet for the wedding. When she brought this up to Eriq, he acted evasive and made excuses, saying that it takes time. Jackie didn't take any of this lightly because she felt that in time, she would lose Eriq if they weren't married. After all, he was handsome.

Eriq did love Jackie. However, as a man who enjoyed being a bachelor, he liked the freedom and outside attention, and did not want that to end just yet. At the same time, he knew he would make a good husband and was aware that children grow up fast, and that his son needed a mother figure—someone who loved him as her own, and who he wouldn't have a problem calling "Mommy." A child needs both a mother and father in the house for full development in life, he thought. From looking closely at the situation, Eriq began to wonder how he would have turned out had he been raised by a single parent.

As he thought these things through, he then understood the importance of this matter and realized it was now time for him to stop procrastinating and devote his attention to the wedding. He didn't really have any savings put away for the event, so he decided to start saving. In addition, he looked into wedding halls, possible tuxes, and various other things. As he did this, everything started to fall into place, so setting a date all of the sudden became easy.

Once everything was set in motion, it took a total of five months before the wedding ceremony finally took place. The mass was held in the same Baptist Church that the Buher family had always attended. It was beautiful. A lot of people from

Eriq's family came. Jackie's guests consisted of Miss Jacobs and a few friends from work. But the number one person Jackie kept thinking about was Mandi. Without her, the wedding just was not complete. If only Mandi could see her now, Jackie would be satisfied. She wouldn't ask for anything else.

Jackie also thought of her mother, Brenda. Even though she was deceased, Jackie often wondered what her mother's reaction would be to suddenly see her little girl married to the man she loved; an accomplishment Brenda herself never achieved. Hopefully, Brenda would be proud. At this time, Eriq was now 27, Jackie was 24, and Preston was the ring bearer, at age 6. The wedding itself wasn't very lavish, but one could tell that money was definitely invested to some extent. Jackie put in what savings she had, Eriq did the same, and Eriq's parents covered what was left, as they had a lot of savings from investments they had made throughout the years.

During the wedding, the two exchanged their own personal vows through letters they each wrote. Anyone listening to the words couldn't help but shed a tear. After the wedding, the couple went off together outside as people threw rice at them. They then hopped into a limousine and travelled to a nearby hotel to freshen up and get ready for the party. On the back of the limo was a sign that read *"Eriq and Jackie Forever."* They were now husband and wife, Mr. and Mrs. Buher. Preston, on the other hand, stayed behind with his grandparents.

The reception was gorgeous. The dance hall had fresh wood floors. The tables all were covered with white cloth and special napkins that looked like teepees. Glasses were already placed at each setting. There were professional decorations of white and silver balloons and colorful designs with messages that said *Just Hitched* or *Eriq Weds Jackie.* And at the far end of the hall was a long table with drinks and all kinds of special appetizers. This was the area in which only the bride, groom and close family members sat.

When Eriq and Jackie arrived, there was massive cheering and celebration. Jackie looked lovely, wearing a white wedding gown and a pearl necklace that Martha lent her. Meanwhile, Eriq looked flawless in his tuxedo—a pure stud. Soon after, the DJ began speaking into the microphone in accordance to the program that was written on the pamphlets. The food was terrific. It consisted of items that were similar to what Eriq's parents served at their house at the Independence Day picnic when Jackie met his family. Along with that menu were delicious cupcakes and ice cream. There was a lot of dancing.

During each dance, Eriq would hold Jackie by the waist as the two just glided side-to-side staring into each other's eyes. In the background, the DJ played all kinds of love songs from artists like Marvin Gaye, Barry White, Luther Vandross and many others. It was a magical night. Of all the songs they enjoyed, the couple's favorite was *Power of Love* by Luther Vandross. After the wedding, the couple prepared to go on their honeymoon in Miami, Florida. They spent a lot of time at the beach, took a few tours, and dined at a few fancy restaurants. The two of them never wanted the moment to end. They went swimming, jogging, and walking along the beach.

At night, they would sit against a palm tree on the beach, feeling the cool breeze rush against their bodies as the waves of the water flowed back and forth. Eriq would be sitting on the beach, leaning against a tree, while Jackie lay on top of him, staring at the moon. Eriq would then caress her hair and body, and each would just stare at the sky for hours, during which they would begin talking about their dreams and goals and love for one another. These moments were magical. Never in a million years would Jackie have ever guessed that this was what love could truly be. To actually be with someone you love, who loves you back, was a feeling one could not put into words. If one had not experienced such, he could only imagine instead of understand.

When they arrived back to Detroit, they returned to Eriq's apartment. It was a one-bedroom unit, which Eriq had lived in for almost two years. Jackie had already moved her things there. She was still a waitress at the restaurant and Eriq still trained at the gym. Even though they were both used to their usual duties by now, it wasn't long before their daily routines and hours conditioned them to not have much time for each other. They were either too exhausted, or worked hours that just weren't convenient for spending time together.

Within three months into their marriage, Jackie discovered she was pregnant. She was so excited. Eriq was happy too. It had always been her dream. She now had life in her belly that she was going to cater to, nurture, love and support. It was the most joyous thing imaginable. Of course, she playfully winked at Eriq with a smile, saying, "Now that's four more to go."

Eriq would laugh and reply, saying, "If we can afford it."

With a child coming, they thought that it would be a good idea to get a bigger place. If they did find one, Jackie wanted to get a bedroom, where she could paint the walls and add all kinds of decorations just for the baby. There was going to be a crib, toys and all the infant items that she wanted.

Lucky for her, one of her co-workers introduced them to their father's house, which had two bedrooms and two bathrooms, a furnished basement and a small garage, and was in a nice neighborhood. Jackie and Eriq arranged for a meeting with the owner and instantly fell in love with it. It wasn't long before they moved in, got situated, and began painting the walls and decorating the baby's room.

Soon after, the ninth month came around. Jackie was already on leave from work and one night began having contractions. She was rushed to the hospital where she was going to have the baby. She was in labor for ten hours before it was finally time to deliver. Jackie had pushed and pushed with Eriq by her side holding her hand.

"Aaaaaaaaaaaaaaaaaaahh!!!" she screamed.

"Again," a nurse instructed.

"Aaaaaaaaaaaaaaaaaaaaaaaaaaaaaaaaaaaaaah!!!!"

This continued on a few more times until finally, it was over. Beside Jackie lay a new baby girl. When Jackie saw her, all she could do was cry. The baby was so beautiful. She had

Jackie's eyes and nose. From Eriq, the happy father, came the girl's dimples.

It was at that point Jackie instantly fell in love. She adored the baby so much that when it was finally time to give the baby a name, all Jackie could think of was *Precious*. And indeed she was. The baby weighted 8 pounds and 11 ounces. It wasn't long before Preston, Justin and the rest of the Buher family came to the hospital to visit, take pictures, and welcome their newest family member. After three days had passed, Eriq eventually wheeled Jackie out of the hospital and into the car as she held Precious in her arms. She was now a full-fledged mother.

9

Broken Glass

L IFE WAS REALLY CHALLENGING FOR ERIQ AND JACKIE now that Precious had been born. Since they both worked, they had to find a proper daycare for their newborn. With childbirth came endless responsibilities such as diapers, wipes, baby milk, bottles, feeding—and sleepless nights, which was a whole new experience for Jackie. All this was accomplished along with supporting Preston. And to handle all these tasks, more money was required. But since the family was below the modest income level, they easily qualified for daycare vouchers and food stamps as a means of support.

Within months, the couple was awarded those benefits, which did provide some room for saving, but very little. However, due to these new responsibilities, Jackie began working longer hours at the restaurant, while Eriq took on a second job working nights at a local gas station. As time progressed, they became more distant from each other as far as spending time as a family. Both had either no time for the other, or the stress from work coupled with the support of the children caused bickering between them. Each spouse was going their own way, so that when they did find time together, they were often at loss for words or too tired.

It took Jackie a while to recognize that something was wrong. She did not feel the same joy that she and Eriq shared before marriage. It was as if everything just stopped being fun anymore. Before they were a pair, Eriq would call her every day, but now it was just twice a week. Living together didn't cut it when there was no communication. And this in turn hurt Jackie. She really wanted to rekindle that flame.

She then thought about Mandi and wondered what her secret was in having a happy and successful marriage. Throughout the time she was seeing Mandi, Jackie would often hear Mandi brag about her family and the joy they all shared together. After thinking for a few moments, she remembered an item that she had overlooked before; one that had been very powerful in bringing her to the place she was now. And that item was her goal book; the very first gift that Mandi ever gave her.

So in dire desperation, Jackie began searching throughout the house for it. She went through the study shelf and drawers and couldn't find it. She searched the entire basement and finally found it in a box that they used for moving, a year ago. The notebook was still clean and intact. Jackie flipped through the pages, reading all the dreams she had written down during the earlier years. She then paused and thought about how many of those dreams came to light.

Then, after spending an hour digesting everything, it became clear. She had stopped dreaming. The books she read were no longer re-read or used as references. Rather than fueling her mind with inspirational material, she fueled it with entertainment such as talk shows and movies that she would watch whenever she returned home from work. And she remembered Mandi reminding her to continue dreaming. And it was not just Mandi saying it, it was a principle suggested in almost all the books Jackie had read.

For instance, in the book, *The Law of Success in Sixteen Lessons*, Napoleon Hill stressed clearly that out of the 16 laws to success, the most important one was having a definite chief aim or definiteness of purpose. For anything to be accomplished, one had to know first where he's going. This was the reason Mandi gave Jackie those books; so they would always be her guide to achieving her goals and bettering herself as a person.

What Mandi gave her were the real keys to success. Each item was very essential because it was almost impossible for Jackie to obtain the accurate ingredients anywhere else. The media, news, school systems, and other forms of information provided misdirection, confusion, and in most cases, endless lies as far as the real secrets to success. Just as the elite tried to conceal the real secrets back in the early 1900s, it was still being done in the mainstream, making it almost impossible to find the right sources out there that would share such information. They just weren't there!

Therefore, it was now up to Jackie to change her thought patterns and have a goal she wanted to pursue. Now, she could have written in her goal book that she wanted an exciting marriage. That would have been fine, but that was too broad. What was required to make it exciting? The answer was "time," she thought. She then took it a step further and asked herself, "What, then, is required to make more time?"

The answer was simple: money. She needed money, money and more money. And she knew from the beginning that the lifestyle she and Eriq were living wasn't in a million years going to generate the kind of freedom they wanted, which is a combination of unlimited time, unlimited money and unlimited security. And that was a commodity very few people could ever boast of having.

Those who had a lot of time, no money, and no security, consisted usually of the unemployed or homeless person. Those who had a lot of money, little time, and no security were usually the specialists: such as doctors, lawyers, business owners, engineers, accountants and other professionals. These kinds of people could own their own practice or business, but in time, that practice or business they think they own, owns them. And if anything happens to them, the income disappears.

And of course, those who had a lot of time, a lot of money, but no security, was the average drug dealer or person engaged in crime for hire in order to make a living. The only problem was that their chances of ending up in prison or death were always enormously higher than the average person's. Plus, as Jackie had learned early on, a lifestyle that harms society will only add more harm, not joy, as evidenced from Peanut who lost her life along with every passenger in her car that fateful day.

But to have all three elements: time, money and security, was golden. And it was not because it sounded nice that compelled Jackie to venture off into that area—although it did sound nice. It was that she didn't want to continue on as a waitress for the rest of her life. She didn't want Eriq to have to work two jobs and not be around. She wanted her husband back where the two of them could share fun and adventure as when they were dating. She missed those times. She believed very strongly that marriage didn't have to be a burden, since it was the joy that compelled both of them to be together in the first place. And lastly, if the couple was going to continue on as strangers in the marriage, what would their future be like in the next five, 10 or 15 years if they even remained together that long? And how would their children respond?

There have been countless studies that have revealed that 90% of all divorces are the result of the stress generated from the lack of time, money or both. And if a person were to study every argument among spouses to determine the root cause, they would find that it most likely stems from one of those three areas.

For instance, if a woman complains how often her husband comes late to pick her up, it's a result of lack of money. Why? Well, if there were already two functioning cars for the couple to drive, then that conversation would have never occurred. One needs money in order to survive and live comfortably. So whoever said that money wasn't important, just didn't have any. Period.

Besides, in the book: *The Science of Getting Rich*, the author, Wallace Wattles, applauded wealth and made it adamantly clear that an abundance of money was essential for human life, and it was the true method for one achieving their full potential in life, since having it creates so many opportunities and things for mankind—if used properly.

All of these factors began registering in the back of Jackie's head throughout the entire morning, so she stayed there thinking about her family, which lasted a few more hours until the early afternoon. That's when she made the decision to start dreaming again, but for better things. She had the husband, the job, the car and the family. Now it was time to upgrade.

Maybe having a bigger house with multiple rooms would be nice. Probably affording a luxury cruise vacation with the family, or driving a more expensive car that was more stylish and secure. But most importantly, it was the lifestyle of having all the time and money she could ever imagine; to have the freedom to spend time with her husband again; to raise her daughter in a safer environment; to have the tools and freedom to create goodness for others; to do what she loved and love what she did.

Jackie began thinking about these things which mirrored the pictures she had attached to her goal book from years ago. Now it was time for her to start believing in them and to become passionate about them.

It was at this moment that she recognized what had happened. The universe had always been working. It's just that since Jackie had not stressed goals as she did in the past, the universe just remained idle, allowing her to live the routine she had been living all this time. Since it hadn't received any command with strong intention, how could it operate any differently? The universe will only do what one commands it to do, through thoughts. That's it. It is immune to sympathy. In fact, it doesn't even know what sympathy means. Only humans do.

So all of a sudden, Jackie began to think of money. She cut out pictures of money and attached them to her notebook. Also, she began drawing designs of dollar bills with specific amounts of what she wanted to have, such as $10 million or $100 million. There was even a $1 billion bill that she wrote twice. If she didn't want to put any more pictures of money in her notebook, she then put them on the walls and doors of her rooms as a reminder whenever she walked by, to think of money. In her car, she hung an air freshener designed like a $100 bill on her rearview mirror. Eriq, who wasn't really interested in knowing about the law of attraction, thought Jackie was crazy, and threatened to take all the pictures down. But Jackie assured him that he would thank her later.

Jackie also went to a few car dealerships to select the car she would drive once she had the money. She was allowed to touch the car and go inside, feeling the leather interior, wood grain, and smelling the newness of the car. She had even asked the salesman to take a picture of her beside the car, which he gladly did, thinking that a customer with this kind of passion would certainly bring him a nice commission.

"Here's my card ma'am. You come see me when you're ready to buy," he'd say with eagerness.

Jackie was, of course, delighted.

The same applied to jewelry and clothing. She would go into the malls and try on clothes and have her friends take pictures of her. As for jewelry, she would try on pieces and snap a picture, promising the store owner she'd return soon to buy them. She was that kind of woman—a fearless person. And as for expensive homes, she would take a short drive, riding past wealthy estates from time to time, envisioning the type of home she would want to live in. It was exciting to her. She also collected a few travel brochures that had pictures of exotic locations that she wanted to travel to, first class, of course.

To actually engage in physically feeling the items that Jackie desired was a powerful technique in attracting that which she wanted. This technique would also make it happen faster, since the universe was also working through the feelings. Feelings start with thought. But when feelings are created through the personal reaction one gets from the perceptions of smell, touch, sound and sight, they become more powerful since it's a true indication of what one wants or doesn't want. Incidentally, it was an exercise that Mandi suggested she do as often as possible.

Now granted all of these activities did not just occur during the first week or first month. It took four months for Jackie to instill all these images in her book and feel them with her hands. But it was definitely the right route to gaining what she wanted. Throughout of all this excitement, Jackie, however, did not know just how she was going to get the money. Of course she could have played the lottery, but she didn't play nor believe in it. To her, spending money on lottery tickets had about the same value as flushed dollar bills down the toilet—a pure waste of time.

But what innovative means could she take on to make more money? She thought and thought. Whatever it was, she knew enough to know that it had to be something that she could own, like a business—on the condition that she would own it and it wouldn't own her. For a moment, she thought of going back to school and taking some business classes. But since she didn't have a GED or high school diploma, she wasn't really interested in going through all the hassles to get the certifications needed to enter into a business program.

She then tried to think of a trade or hobby she was skilled in. She was a great writer of stories and poetry, but she did not see that as having any real impact, financially. So she then thought of writing a book on the law of attraction, but it was a subject that appeared too complex for her to explain through writing at the present moment. So, she remained at a standstill. All she knew was that if she was going to be financially independent, she had to have something unique.

Two weeks passed and still no idea came along; yet she did not let it discourage her. For she knew a *way* would be granted.

Then, on a cool Monday afternoon, she went to her car to pick up Preston from school. But for some reason, her car didn't start. She saw that the lights on the dashboard didn't appear and thus assumed that the battery was probably weak or disconnected. She went around to pop the hood and tried moving the clamps with her hands, but both ends seemed tight. She then tried starting the car again, but it still didn't start. There was virtually no sound when twisting the key and everything on the dashboard remained dark. So, she concluded she needed a jump start. She had jumper cables, but Eriq was at work. So she had to search for a neighbor or someone who was willing to bring their car to her so that she could jump start her car. She walked past a few houses and noticed no cars in the driveways. No one was home. She then went in the opposite direction, and saw cars parked in each of the next three houses, but two of the neighbors didn't answer, and the other made an excuse, claiming that he was too tired.

Jackie then got frustrated and went back to her car, closed the hood, threw the cables in the backseat and slammed the door. Without knowing what else to do, she looked in her purse, saw there was money in it, and hopped on a bus to pick up Preston. Fortunately, she wouldn't have to pick up Precious from daycare for a few hours. By then, she thought she would finally receive help for her car.

When she arrived at the school, she was already late. Most of the kids had already left and Preston was sitting along with some other students in the office. By this time, he was now in third grade. Jackie apologized to the staff for the delay. They accepted and gave her a sheet of paper to sign showing Preston was picked up. Jackie signed it and the two of them left the school.

As they approached the bus stop, Preston suddenly broke away from Jackie's hand, insisting that they walk home instead.

"Why do you want us to walk?" she asked him.

Preston looked at her with an open smile. "All the parents walk their kids. Besides, it's really not that far."

Suddenly, Preston started toward the street while the light in front of him was still green, signaling him to cross, which he did as Jackie chased him across the street. Preston still kept running down the sidewalk, past a few houses. Jackie, who now was slightly overweight, was in absolutely no mood to start running. So she demanded that he stop.

Preston then looked at her. "What? I just wanted to show you I know the way home," he said.

"I know," she said panting slightly. "But that does not mean you leave me. If you want… we'll walk home. Just don't ever run from me again. You got that?"

Preston agreed and the two of them began walking home. Though, this would be the first time they had ever walked together from school. Their house was just a mile and a half away, but due to the fact that Jackie was always on her feet at work, she just never thought of using them to pick up Preston or drop him off.

Upon reaching the halfway point to their house, they observed a few boys circling around another house, giggling.

"Look Mom," Preston pointed.

"Yeah, I know," Jackie answered "But let's keep going."

The little boys were about 40 feet away from them, but as Jackie and Preston proceeded, the distance between them got shorter and shorter. The two boys were still running along the driveway and onto the porch. They peeked inside the house and saw that no one was there. So they ran from the porch and around to the side of the house, then threw a brick through the window, out of mischief. Both Jackie and Preston heard the glass shatter because, at this moment, they were now in front of the driveway of the house, where the two boys eventually scrambled off, laughing.

Jackie looked at the house for a moment and out of curiosity went to the side to check the damage. She then looked at the rest of that side of the house before finally looking at Preston, who was still standing on the sidewalk. "Come here," she whispered. Preston came beside her.

Now, if one were to ask Jackie what compelled her to want to suddenly check inside that house, she wouldn't know what to say. All she knew was that some mysterious voice kept telling her to go in, and so she did.

"Just wait here," she whispered to Preston. "I'll be right back." Preston nodded.

She then reached over and lifted the frame of the other window that wasn't broken. It was already half open, thus enabling her to easily enter inside. She climbed on a small platform and lifted her body weight inside before pushing herself onto the floor of the house. She knew this was illegal, and risky, and not a good example for Preston. But some impulse kept telling her to go in there. She wasn't going to stay long. She just wanted to take a quick look.

When she got in, she immediately saw the brick that was on the floor along with broken glass around it. She moved into what appeared to be the living room. She turned and studied the walls and saw that there were no holes or dents in them. However, the walls did need painting. She then turned and went to the kitchen that had solid tiles and a sink still intact. She tried to turn on the faucet, but there was no water. The countertop was still in place and the cabinets, though old, were still attached firmly to the walls.

She continued down the hallway and saw a bathroom on the left hand side which also seemed undisturbed. The toilet, sink, bathtub and shower faucet were all in place, but the floor was missing two ceramic tiles. Across from the bathroom was one bedroom, which was entirely neat. After a quick glance around, she went upstairs to what appeared to be three more bedrooms, all of which seemed in good condition. The floor of the entire house was covered with old blue carpet, which definitely needed to be replaced.

After observing the upstairs for a few minutes, she went down to the basement. The basement was dirty. Dirt was everywhere on the floor. Though, it still had a washer and a dryer line hookup. A gas meter and water meter were located at the far end of the wall, along with a hot water tank that was not too far from it. The only thing missing was a furnace. It was gone. Soon, Jackie went back up to the first floor and took one more quick glance at the kitchen and living room before finally escaping back through the side window. Thankfully Preston was still there, waiting. Jackie was relieved.

"C'mon," she said with a smile. "Let's go home."

But, before they were completely off the premises, Jackie made sure to write down the address of the house.

As soon as they got home, Jackie began thinking about the house. The house was not in bad shape. There was not too much major repair required except the replacement of the carpet, painting of the walls, and installation of a new furnace. Also, the basement needed a thorough clean up. Besides that, there was really nothing else wrong with the place.

But there was just some mystery about that house that Jackie couldn't figure out. All she had was the address. So she decided that if anything, she would investigate to find out more about the house. Maybe that might clear up the mystery.

She didn't know where to go to find more information, but after asking a few people during the week, she finally found out where to go, and that was the County Recorder's Office. It was where the entire history of all residential properties within the county were listed. One could find out when the house was first built, who owns the house, the area of the house, whether it had back taxes… and a whole lot more.

So Jackie went there to find out about the house. Again, she didn't know why she was doing this except that there was just something she needed to know. Once she pulled up the information, she then printed it out, which, at $2 a page, cost her about $6. What she found out was interesting.

The house was owned by a man who lost his job. It was bought and paid for. However, he owed three years of property taxes on it. Because he had not made the tax payments, the government took the property, thereby forcing him to leave. Therefore, the house had a tax lien on it. And in effect, the house was going to go into a sale auction.

After studying the history, Jackie then went to the office to ask questions regarding tax liens and auctions. By the time she gathered the information, a sudden feeling came over her, and she decided to attend the auction. From that thought came the idea of possibly owning a home or multiple homes just like that one for income. The idea was simple. Just purchase the home at a tax lien rate, fix it up, then get renters to live there. "Why didn't I think of this all along?" she kept wondering.

From that point on, it was obvious. She had found her calling. She decided to engage in real estate. She didn't know how that would occur or if she needed any money. All she knew was that real estate was going to be her trade. From wherever she was now, she was going to make something out of it—someway, somehow. The only hope was that she would turn it into something big, like an empire. And again, she wasn't familiar with any of the tax laws or codes or how business was done. All she knew was that she was going to go into real estate and that was final.

On that same night while driving home, Jackie suddenly heard an ad on the radio, inviting people to come to a training seminar on real estate, which ironically came right after R. Kelly's song, *"I Believe I Can Fly"* finished playing. In the ad was a promotion on the various ways a person could make money as a real estate investor. As soon as she began hearing this, she pulled the car over to write down the number of the company. The invitation was free. What was interesting was that this program was renowned nationwide, but was actually coming to town in a week for a limited time. All she had to do was call and reserve her seat. After stopping to write down the number, she immediately drove home.

As soon as she got home, she called for a reservation. She was so thrilled and excited with the offer. She knew that there would eventually be a charge of some sort, but felt in her bones that this was the right thing to do. For her to feel this excited after looking into an abandoned house would probably never have occurred if her car had started. That was clear. And, thanks to Preston running away from her as he did, so that they wouldn't take the bus, they walked past this house. That also helped a lot. So in her mind, this was what the universe was showing her to do to make money. No other venture idea had given her this kind of excitement.

When Eriq arrived late, Jackie went on to explain the program and all the events that transpired within the past few days that led her to this point. Eriq wasn't too impressed. To him, Jackie tended to make poor decisions at times and make conclusions without carefully thinking things through. As a result, he just encouraged her to go to the seminar, but to not pay for anything until they talked it over first. Jackie agreed, out of respect for her husband's wishes. After all, she had not made any poor decisions since she had met this man.

As soon as Wednesday came around, Jackie went to the hall of a local hotel where the seminar was being held. There was a table set up with pamphlets and books on one side, and on the other side of the room was a long table with a big pitcher of ice water beside several glasses for people to help themselves. Jackie had brought a notebook and a blue pen with her. She couldn't wait. As soon as it started, a middle-aged man who appeared to be the speaker began talking about the program and what it was intended to do.

He gave insight on the differences between a job versus a business, as well as the benefit of home ownership, as it relates to the banks and personal cash flow. Jackie was absorbing every detail. The seminar lasted for about 90 minutes. Following, there was the invitation to engage in the training—for a price. The charge was $600. And it had to be made that day, at that event, because of the nature of the program moving to different cities. With the price came exercise materials, such as tapes and videos, as well as notebooks that were required to takes notes and make calculations during the exercises.

Jackie was slightly hesitant. She didn't know it was going to be that expensive. And it wasn't her fault, because that was how most of these seminars were set up. The price was always the last thing discussed. However, this training program was highly reputable and known for producing a number of millionaires in real estate. So its credibility was no question. The question was whether Jackie had the money. In this case, she did and she didn't.

Both she and Eriq had a joint checking account where they could make withdrawals and deposits at will. This was their main account from which all expenses were paid. Therefore, they had to be careful about their expenses to ensure that checks didn't bounce and there were no overdraft fees. They each had savings accounts, but very little was ever in those. With that said, there was no other means that Jackie knew of right now to pay for the training. So she decided to make the payment using their checking account.

Now, the good part was that money was in the account. The only problem was that it was the exact amount needed to pay the rent, which was due the following week. She knew that this would hurt Eriq greatly if she spent the money. She also remembered the promise she made to Eriq to discuss the matter before she paid for anything. But she also believed in her heart that he would not support her anyway in entering the program, which was what she wanted to do.

She knew she was going to hear from him after she did this, but in her mind, this just had to be done. The hell with the consequences. She was centered on greatness, and to her, how does one become great without taking risks? This attitude stemmed from books she read, like *Think and Grow Rich* by Napoleon Hill and *How I Raised Myself from Failure to Success in Selling* by Frank Bettger. One had to take risks in life. Besides, being great didn't require permission. One just had to go out and do it, and her time was NOW. Procrastinating over it was never going to get it done. Such was also explained in *The Magic of Thinking Big* by David Schwartz.

As explained in *Think and Grow Rich*, so many people go about life without knowing exactly what it is they want or where they're going, and allow others to do the decision-making for them. But in order to know what one wants or know where one is going, one had to have a chief aim of their own and be able to make solid decisions effectively. Such tools, which are very valuable and vital for any person, are rarely if at all discussed or encouraged in schools or colleges, which is why the majority of students coming out of college seek any job that's offered to them as a means of stability rather than as a tool towards attaining their ultimate goal in life, if at all they have one.

Opinions are like intestines. Everyone has one, but sometimes, they can also be full of… well, crap. They can never measure a person's tenacity, nor provide an accurate chance at a person's success. And right now, Jackie was in a successful mindset. She knew she could do this. She didn't want to move backwards in life anymore, by living in fear of what could go wrong. She had come so far, and wanted to continue to move forward, and moving forward in this case meant being financially free. She had a dream; a desire; a mission and she was going to achieve it by all means, provided it was legal. So with the stroke of a pen, she wrote the check out to *Metzer's Home Investor Academy*, which was the name of the company. She then received the materials and was given the date of the first training session. It was a five-day session from 8 a.m. to 4 p.m., Monday through Friday at another hotel, which would begin in three weeks. Jackie would have to work those days, but would arrange something with Pacco, her boss, to make the seminar. She was so excited and sang the entire way home.

That night, she cooked Eriq dinner while waiting to tell him the news. As outspoken as she was, she figured it was best he knew now, rather than later. She truly did feel bad about going back on her word, but she would not add to that emotion by being dishonest. She would tell him everything. When he arrived, he appeared very tired and exhausted. He was just coming from his job at the gas station, which began only an hour after he finished his other job at the gym. As soon as he closed the door, he dropped his keys on the table and began surfing through the mail that came that day.

"Hey baby," he said. "What'ch you doin' up?"

"Um, I made the spaghetti you always like and have something I wanna tell you," Jackie replied.

She was sitting on her ankles on top of the couch, in a yoga position.

At this moment, Eriq was now anxious about what Jackie had to tell him, especially since Jackie had never positioned herself that way before. "What, you're pregnant again?" he asked.

"No," she giggled.

"Is there another guy?" he joked again.

"*No*," she remarked again.

"Okay, well how are the kids?"

"They're fine, sleeping."

"Okay then. Well it can't be that bad. Just give me a minute."

After he was done skimming through the mail, Eriq flung the entire batch back on the table as he got it. He then went to hang up his jacket. After a few minutes, he returned back to Jackie. The spaghetti was still hot, so Eriq had a little time to wait.

"Okay. So what do you want to talk to me about?"

Before Jackie could speak, she bit her bottom lip, closed her eyes. "Now I know you're going to get mad at this... *but...* I bought the program."

At that instant, she quickly moved from the couch and stood up next to a wall, knowing she was going to be chewed out.

"What? I... I thought we agreed you wouldn't do anything without asking... "

"I know. I know. But baby you weren't there and I had to make this move or else I couldn't get into the program. And I really want to be in that training."

Eriq looked at her carefully. "How much was it?" he asked.

"Six hundred," she replied, coughing.

"Dollars?"

Jackie nodded slowly.

"From which account?"

"Our... joint checking," she coughed again, patting her chest.

"No... no... you didn't. How are we going to pay our rent?"

"Please don't worry. I'll cover it up. Don't be upset. This thing is really important to me... "

"How? How... are you going to cover it?"

"Baby you got to understand," she pleaded. "I don't want to live this way anymore."

"Like what?"

"Like this. I mean we barely have time for each another. You work two jobs. And I'm tired of always being on my feet as a waitress. Trust me. The love affair is not there. Something has got to change. I just want something *more*. I can no longer go about my life wondering what I could have been than what I am now. I want us to be together. What about the things we said we'd do or the places we wanted to go see or... "

"Or what? You think some fucking real estate course is going to help with that?"

"Yes. I really do," Jackie said with confidence.

Eriq then pointed at her. "You know, you're really crazy, you know that? You're mental. I mean here I am busting my ass for this family, making the most money in this house, and you're here treating it like it ain't shit!" At this time, Eriq's voice got real loud. "You don't make shit at your job. I'm the one making almost all the money and all I hear is that you have this hunch for a fucking dream that hasn't even come into light! You think you can just use me like that? What kind of person do you think I am? Huh? What kind of person?"

At this very moment, Eriq was in rage and approached Jackie violently, pushing her hard to the wall. Instantaneously, that action drew flashbacks in Jackie's mind of the past abuse she endured when as a little girl and she soon broke down in tears.

"You... get your hands off of me. You hear me?!" she screamed, shaking herself. "GET OFF ME! *Don't* touch me."

Eriq immediately withdrew his hands. Jackie then walked one step to regain her balance. With tears still strolling down her cheeks, she looked at him straight in the eye.

"Eriq. Don't you ever put your hands on me like that again! You don't ever want to see the old "Jackie" come out, because believe me, when it comes out, even *I* will be stunned by the result, which will happen right before I call the cops and paramedics. The cops will be for taking me in while the paramedics will be for putting you on a stretcher right before rushing you straight to intensive care. So you better have your insurance card ready! Trust me, you haven't seen me in action and I'm sure you don't want to. You're free to disagree with me in any decision I make as much as you want, but don't you *dare* in your life touch me that way again... EVER! You got that?"

With nothing else to say, Eriq went back to his room to get his jacket.

"Just know we're changing that account. There no longer will be a joint account between us. From now on, you're on your own," he said with a soft voice. "Fuck it. I don't care anymore."

At that moment, he shut the door and drove off to get some air, leaving the spaghetti untouched. Though, there was no way of telling just how long he would be gone. What was clear was that he no longer was interested in eating any dinner for the night. So, it was now better off in the fridge. All Jackie could do now was lay down in her bed and cry. Her only hope was that she made the right decision and this plan worked. Then, due to the commotion, Precious suddenly began crying as well.

10

≈◇≈

Real Estate Delight

Jackie was getting ready for the training. Eriq eventually apologized to her for his actions and the two of them made amends. They were, however, short on the rent since that argument. Jackie gave what she could muster up from her job, which was half of the rent. Though she assumed full responsibility and told the landlord that the rest of the money would be made up before the following week. The next week Jackie fulfilled her word. By this time now, Preston was approaching 9 years old and Precious had celebrated her first birthday.

At this time also, papers arrived from the court regarding Preston. Sophia was demanding joint custody. After several years of non-existence, Sophia suddenly wanted to be in Preston's life, which, according to the State, was permitted based upon her progress in the drug rehabilitation program. She had been clean for several months and was working now, and appeared stable.

Yet, Eriq wasn't convinced of the change and was going to fight with every bone in his body to ensure Preston remained with him. He really couldn't verify Sophia's overall condition and the last thing he ever wanted was for Preston to be corrupted by her. Preston, who basically didn't know Sophia, wanted, of course, to stay where he was, and Eriq's parents were 100% in support of this. There was no question that Preston was receiving all the love and support he could from his family. However, he was still Sophia's son and she wanted to see him before it got to a point when he was unaware that she ever existed.

From that perspective everyone, including Jackie, could understand. However, it was still going to be a battle between both sides, and the court would eventually determine the result as far as custody issues went. Though, this case was going to drag on for months before anything would ever be resolved. So the Buher family had some time to prepare their case which, of course, was going to require some money for a good lawyer.

Meanwhile, when the following week came, Jackie was up early and ready to attend her class. With her, she carried reading glasses and the notebooks required for the course. She listened to a few of the tapes and watched the video. She found them both to be very interesting and was very eager to learn more in order to apply the principles to real life.

When she got there, she noticed that there were many people attending. The large hall was full of people of all different nationalities and ethnic groups. She found a seat and greeted the people at her table. There was loud commotion everywhere that continued on for another 15 minutes before the training began. By the time the teacher finally began to speak, everything was quiet. However, it wasn't the same person who Jackie met at the seminar. This person was different. He was a Caucasian male who used to be a law professor, who had retired after a few years of using the techniques taught in the program. He, too, had been a student just like those present in the class that day. His total net worth was a little over a million dollars, thereby qualifying him to teach.

After finishing a brief history about himself, he asked some members of the audience why they were in this training and what they expected to acquire from it. While there was a lot of variance in the details of their answers, the overall theme suggested that they all wanted freedom, just like Jackie. Throughout the entire five-day training, the teacher, who was an exceptionally gifted speaker, showed them 11 ways to make money in real estate. There were issues such as foreclosures on residential and commercial properties, tax liens, motor homes, empty lots, buyback options and a whole lot more. Under these parameters were different situations offered to create calculations for different returns on property investing.

The class also dealt with the methods in which to negotiate with banks or debtors; the difference between a traditional and nontraditional lender; and which one to pick for a specific deal. There also were ways that one could give offers to sellers in order to purchase their home without a lender and still make a return, having no money down. But the very first point that the instructor stressed was that a person had to set up a corporation and have at least decent credit, and offered several reasons to back that up. He also stressed the importance of having the business set up as either an LLC or incorporation, and went over the different tax benefits of each option. Credit was very important, because that was what each individual needed in order to establish bank credit and other factors. So the instructor suggested that each individual check his or her credit score with the three main credit bureaus to determine whether it was at least 700 or better.

In addition to the class, real estate experts were available on the premises who could answer questions regarding almost any other issue relating to real estate or credit. After each training session, Jackie would get tired. There was just so much to learn, in a very short, fast-paced time frame. When she got home, she would conduct different exercises to make sure she grasped the concepts. Then she would take a short nap, and get right back to the assignments and exercises when she awoke, after, of course, looking at all the pictures of money she had taped to her walls. Inside she smiled, just knowing that her day would come for financial freedom. She went through this routine every day.

During the sessions, the teacher explained that the class was just an introduction to the methods of real estate investing and that the program also had a staff of mentors and professional investors who would work one-on-one with each student to ensure that they mastered different aspects of real estate investing. The goal was for each student to eventually conduct their own real estate business out in the real world. They were to observe and study the history of hundreds of homes within a month before carefully choosing two or three deals they felt could bring in a profit. If done right, the minimum profit each student could earn off of one deal could be at least $20,000, depending on the value of the home and what kind of deal it was. Those profits would then be used as capital to support the next deal, which would then support the next deal, and so on.

The idea was not to get carried away and spend the money foolishly. It was to be used to support other business deals so that a person could have multiple properties in a matter of months. Jackie liked the idea and was thrilled with the entire philosophy of investing. In her mind, the class was definitely worth the money she paid.

But, as explained earlier, the five-day training program was only meant to offer insight into investment opportunities in real estate that a student could take on if they were interested. And if they wished to continue, there would be another cost. This time, the fee was much higher. The entire cost for the actual training was $10,000. Included in this program were advanced teachers who would teach different investing aspects that the student had to master before earning his or her completion certificate. The program would also guarantee the student's ability to start a corporation. And, after the student graduated, he or she would be assigned a personal mentor who, for 90 days, would oversee the first few deals so as to ensure the quality and effectiveness of the work.

Jackie wasn't sure what kind of credit she had. She knew, however, that she never owned a credit card or had any outstanding bills. She was unfamiliar with the credit system and never had a need to use credit in her life prior to prison. And even though she was now a wife and mother, she still didn't own a credit card. She did get offers in the mail, but they were difficult for her to understand, so she threw them away. All she paid were utility bills, which were all on time as well as the rent she and Eriq shared on the lease.

So, in order to clearly understand where she stood, Jackie went to the back of the hall where a representative was able to pull up her credit score. Not every student did this. Many of them already knew that their score was too low for them to participate in the venture, and thus ignored the option of finding out again.

According to her report, Jackie was in good standing, with an average score of 705. She did have a balance with an auto repair company, regarding a repair that was done on her car, which she was making timely payments on. Otherwise, she did not have much of a credit history. She did get offers in the mail, but they were difficult for her to understand, so she threw them away. All she paid were utility bills, which were all on time as well as the rent she and Eriq shared on the lease.

So, in order to clearly understand what her options were, she was asked to move to another table in the back of the hall. When it was her time to meet with a representative there, she was told that if she wanted to continue with the program, but couldn't afford the entire cost, she was approved for the financing of half of the cost of the training. The first half would come out of her pocket. Therefore, she had to come with $5,000 if she wanted to continue. If she did, the program would begin in three months in Memphis, Tennessee, where the students would spend seven weeks learning strategies of real estate investing.

The students would stay in a cabin not far from where the training took place. Once there, the students would attend classes on the strategies and observe real-life real estate transactions. By the time the program was finished, all students would have become masters on all real estate subjects and professional enough to go out in the world to make deals of their own. And, by having their own corporation, custom-designed business cards, and most importantly, their own mentor, their confidence would be raised so their chance of success was highly likely, provided they remained consistent.

Though, throughout the training, students were still responsible for their own meals and transportation. The fee only included the classes, training and lodging. Jackie decided that this was definitely what she wanted to do. All she had to do was come up with $5,000. The program did stipulate, however, that she had to put $1,000 down within a week to reserve her place and provide the rest two weeks before the training was to begin. Therefore, she had to come up with $4,000 nine weeks after the first deposit. It seemed pretty harsh, but it was clear that there were many expenses involved in the program. The company had to prepare for the event, organize the classes, rent the hall, provide the materials, select and pay for the right teachers, hire the mentors, etc.

Jackie understood all this, and with a smile, she felt confident and believed that somehow, some way, she was entering that class, no matter what. She didn't care if she had to eat and sleep at *Pacco's Kitchen*, she was going to that training. So, after discovering all she needed to know regarding how to enter the program, her five days with this part of the class had ended. Jackie had to figure out what to do now. She knew that she was going to need Eriq's help in order to fund it.

When Eriq arrived home, Jackie told him how the class went and pleaded with him to provide half of the deposit within a week to reserve her spot. Eriq immediately said "no" without thinking about it. Jackie tried to convince him with all the strength in her body, but he still objected and went off to bed.

Jackie had only $387 in her savings account. So, on the following day, she went to her job and begged her boss to let her work the entire week. By now, she had earned a reputation for being very upfront and honest, and Pacco trusted her. So, he allowed her to work as desired without giving it a thought. She was so grateful. And during that week, it was very busy. Even Pacco was surprised. It had been a long time since he witnessed so much activity during the middle of the week. It came to the point when he even asked Jackie to work overtime, and she did.

By the end of the week, she had all the money needed to put down the deposit. During the following week, Pacco called to speak with her in private. It was to give her a promotion. She was selected to be the manager of the restaurant. Therefore, after Pacco, she was next in charge in handling all the inventory, the employees, the money, and other responsibilities that went along with running a restaurant. Pacco had been impressed by Jackie's attitude and had always wanted to give her the position. He was just waiting for the right time. And to him, this was it.

Even though the hours were going to be longer, this was exactly what Jackie needed. And to be given this honor could not have come at a more perfect time. She had exactly six more weeks to come up with $4,000. She knew, however, that this position would be short-lived if she went to Memphis for the training. Yet, she wasn't too concerned about that. She believed that from just obtaining the knowledge and making just one deal, she could establish enough living capital in case she no longer worked there.

Four weeks went by and Jackie was able to accumulate $2,200 to put toward her deposit for her training. She had been working over 50 hours per week. But the excitement she had built, knowing that she had almost saved the deposit, caused her not to feel any exhaustion or stress. In knowing that both Eriq and Jackie were working long hours now, Martha and Ernie took a greater part in picking up Preston from school and caring for baby Precious.

During the entire ordeal, Jackie lost 15 pounds, which was the exact weight she needed to lose to become a perfect size 6, which was what she indirectly wanted anyway. So she was very happy. She now had that same sexy frame that she had when she first met Eriq, and Eriq was pleased with that.

Within two weeks, she earned another $1,100 and put it toward the balance. Yet she was still short by $700. She eventually sold a few items in the house such as a camcorder, her and Eriq's bedroom TV, and pawned a couple of necklaces, leaving her with a difference of $210 to fulfill for the training. To complete that, she borrowed the money from Eriq's parents, promising to pay them back. She was set.

When the program date finally came around, Jackie had to tell Pacco that she needed to take off and that she was not sure if she'd be back, but sincerely thanked him for the entire opportunity.

Pacco, a bit unhappy, accepted her notice and told her "farewell." The two of them shook hands and then hugged. Some of her co-workers were also going to miss her, but this had been Jackie's plan all along and she was now excited for what was ahead.

Eriq ended up driving Jackie to Memphis. When they got there, she found her assigned cabin space and the two of them took a short tour of the school and compound. Within a few short hours, the couple embraced and shared a few words.

"You know I'll miss you," Eriq said.

"I'll miss you too," she replied.

"You take care, okay?" Jackie nodded.

"Just don't forget to call me every day to tell me how you're doing. All right?"

"I won't… and take care of the kids. Okay?"

"You got it. Just remember to leave them fellas alone. I don't want to find out that you're getting more than just a study session."

Jackie started laughing. "And you remember not to give any of them women out there more than just a paid work-out," she joked back.

The two of them laughed. After, Eriq looked into her eyes in a way that he hadn't done since the night they got engaged. He kissed her lightly and told her how proud he was of her and that in spite of everything, deep down he was impressed by her strong will, drive, and determination. That to him symbol-ized a real woman from which he believed something special would come out of all this. And who could argue with that?

Jackie's actions also taught Eriq that everyone came into this world with a purpose. It was just a question of whether that person chose to express that purpose or not. The grave-yard is filled to the brim with countless men and women blessed with so many gifts, which were never exposed while they were on earth. They went throughout life doing noth-ing more with their minds than what they did yesterday and the day before, which was why whatever hidden talents and gifts they did have while on earth, followed them to their grave.

This would then explain, from a spiritual sense, why the graveyard is the richest land on earth instead of the oil wells or diamond mines. It is filled with so many priceless un-knowns. And since those same people died with their talents unexposed, no one will ever truly know who they really were or what they could have become. The more one fits *in* with society, the less he's noticed *by* society. And in life, man is either remembered or forgotten. That's it.

Therefore, Eriq needed to search within his own soul and find out what *his* true calling was. In actuality, he had been too afraid to venture to that point. But based on how bravely Jackie displayed her character, Eriq finally had the inspiration he needed to believe that he, too, could venture off to that point as well, whatever it was. Sometimes, it takes the courage of one individual to inspire others to find their own calling. All it really takes is just a decision, faith— and never, ever letting go, no matter what. And provided that decision is strong, everything else will take care of itself, regardless of what tools the person does or doesn't have with him along the way. Man's duty here on earth is to soar well beyond reason; like a god. The world is always screaming for ideas. Eriq now had to search for what his was. After one final embrace, Eriq got into his car, blew his wife a kiss, and went off. He could see Jackie waving in the rearview mirror as he left.

Her new classes started that evening. For Jackie, it was rigorous, yet interesting. Jackie, who was a fast learner, discovered all kinds of concepts and was taught how to negotiate deals. She eventually set up a corporation, titled *Queen Realty Corp, LLC.*

She chose "Queen" since it was her middle name. She learned about how to earn monthly returns on motor homes and commercial property. There were even sessions where they studied real live scenarios of investors negotiating with banks. The whole emphasis was to be liquid, to where there was enough capital in which a person could make multiple deals that would earn consistent cash flow. Jackie also learned about tax liens and foreclosures, like the house she found with the broken window. After the classes were over for the day, Jackie would either take her materials to the cabin or sit at a public lunch hall, going over problems and rereading the subject matter. She was determined to know the information like the back of her hand. She wanted to know this better than anybody. To her, there was no other option.

As the training progressed, students were told to express the different methods in which to approach a bank, seller or buyer. Jackie did this several times. She made mistakes initially, but eventually, got better. Soon, it became very simple.

By the time the entire training was over, Jackie had learned so much and was so excited with the prospect of making her first deal. She proudly accepted her certificate from the program. On her way back to Michigan, her job was to immediately research homes and select one or two that had the potential of becoming a lucrative transaction. After she did that, she was to do nothing else. All that was required of her was that she contact her assigned mentor, who would then guide her through, step by step, on what to do next. The mentor had a vested interest in seeing her succeed, since he stood to make a 20% commission on her first five deals.

The first couple of months were rough. Jackie, who now was unemployed, was doing this full time. She had no idea the amount of work that was required. Within the first two weeks, Jackie showed very little activity. But it wasn't until she discovered that she had no money to buy even the simplest of things that she suddenly became motivated to work. After a month and half since her return from Memphis, she researched and studied 88 homes from which she obtained two that seemed promising. The goal was for her to obtain at least one house in order to begin, but two was fine.

Her mentor researched the data on the homes and figured them to have profit potential. If the deal for one house went as planned, Jackie's return would be $15,000. It was a little below average, but for a beginner, it wasn't too bad. After a lot of work between her and her mentor, and applying all the information she learned in class, along with a lot of patience, a buyer did make a deal with her and she made a return.

She was so ecstatic. Even Eriq was happy. Although she felt very lucky, she also was wise. She had dedicated her time very passionately and studied very, very hard to be the best. She did what she was taught and used the majority of that return to invest in another property, which eventually yielded $32,000. It was then that her confidence went through the roof. She could do it now. There was no turning back. All she had to do was stay on course.

The biggest reason why many of the students didn't achieve much success in the program was because they allowed their emotions to take over their common sense. Rather than earn and invest, earn and invest, they suddenly would use their earnings to buy commodities, forgetting they still had an obligation to the bank, as far as credit. It wasn't long before their credit suffered and they ended up losing what they had worked so hard to establish. Patience is a virtue and with time, one can enjoy the good life. But very few ever reason that way, let alone apply that principle.

In Jackie's case, she wasn't going to make that mistake. To her, this was the only shot she had. Failure was no option. The criticism that she would endure if she failed was far too great for her to even attempt to think of going off course. If she failed, she would have to hear Eriq say, "I told you so." And if not that, it was back to another dead-end job that offered low wages, no benefits and unlimited resentment. Whenever she saw it in just those terms, it became all the fuel she needed to stay focused. And besides, self discipline was another important law that Napoleon Hill had expressed in his book *The Law of Success in Sixteen Lessons*. And in *The Richest Man in Babylon* by George Clason, which Jackie also read, it discussed the laws of managing money in order to obtain wealth. In essence, its central theme was delay, delay, delay and be patient on the 'good', so that you can enjoy the *great!*

11

❧

Miss Thang

Within six months, Jackie made her first five deals, which earned her a total of $146,223. With that capital, she began diversifying her money in higher valued property that became even more rewarding. She still received coaching from the program, and this helped her decide to find other areas in which to invest that were both smart and lucrative.

And boy, were they ever. They were starting to generate consistent money month after month, long after Jackie had closed the deals. In business, Jackie learned, this was residual income, and it was much like a steady paycheck for entrepreneurs; which meant that it was money that was safe to spend. It wasn't long before such income began paying for all the household expenses.

Eriq eventually quit his job at the gas station and started working part time at the gym. This time, there was nothing he could say. Jackie had won. She had proved him wrong. By the time Jackie's net worth rose to $1 million, he didn't have to work anymore at any gym. It took a little over two years for Jackie to reach such an accomplishment, but in everyone's eyes, it was well worth it. She was now 29, a year before the new millennium.

During the journey, she and Eriq had welcomed twin boys. Their names were Max and Miles, or M&M, as people would say. They were so cute and a dream-come-true for Jackie. To bear multiple children at birth was always something she had heard about. But for her to actually bear them herself felt incredible! Yet she figured it all had a little bit to do with her genetics from her mother's side. Jackie remembered her aunt, Maggie, who was her mother's twin sister, but died in prison of pneumonia shortly before Jackie went to jail.

The last time Jackie ever saw Maggie was when Jackie went to visit her in prison, when she was 16. When Maggie died, Jackie felt like she no longer had anything else to live for. And even if she did, who would care? As a result, fueled by rage, Jackie took part in all kinds of erratic behavior as a means to numb her loneliness and despair. To her, Peanut and Jackie's other friends were okay, but there's a special connection that family blood lines share that just can't be explained or experienced, with even the closest friend. And, no matter how *bad* that family member may be, he or she is still never out of that person's life. Memories of them tend to always resurface in the mind.

But, now that Jackie had her own family, whom she loved, adored and appreciated so much, life suddenly made perfect sense again, for which she was so grateful. She now had more than enough to live for.

Though, family life didn't obstruct Jackie's focus. Along with her new fortune, Jackie became introduced to other investments including high-risk stocks and bonds, offshore banking, trading in foreign currencies, and day trading, which, in turn, increased her net worth to $10 million in two more years, with over a quarter million coming in monthly. And, it was only growing. Yes, it was clear: She had arrived.

Besides Michigan, Jackie had obtained property in Florida, Georgia, California and Texas. Texas was a particularly interesting state because of its motor homes. It was said that owning motor homes was the equivalent to a person having an ATM machine in his backyard. The money just kept flowing in month after month after month. Near all this property were physical offices where she now employed up to 60 people. Soon, Jackie and the family moved to Georgia and lived in a large house not far from a huge vacant land.

As it turned out, Jackie and Eriq ended up purchasing this land to build their dream home. The land was located far into the country side. The location was perfect. It was in an area where they couldn't see any neighbors within a half-mile radius, which was what they wanted. The plan exemplified their pure dream home.

They wanted at least seven bedrooms, four bathrooms, indoor and outdoor swimming pools, a separate guest house, a four-car garage, a mini theatre, an outdoor field for sports, four walk-in closets, an elaborate living room, a big kitchen, a library study, a room for cutting and styling hair, a fitness room, a laundry room, a circular stairway leading to the upstairs, at least four separate balconies, and much more. The carpet in the house, except for the entrance way, had to be Italian.

On the outside of the house would be rosebushes that bordered the entrance way and perimeter of the house. Along with those would be water fountains in both the front and back of the house. They also were going to have a small cabin where they could house at least two horses. And as far as plants went, they would be in the far distant corner of the premises where also peppers, tomatoes, potatoes, onions, carrots, and greens would be grown. And they would plant orange, apple and peach trees close by.

This was what they wanted. According to the architects, the entire plan was going to cost at least $15 million and would take a minimum of six months to complete. Jackie and Eriq weren't worried. But before they even decided to go in that direction, Jackie had accountants and attorneys guide her every step of the way in building the house. It was projected to take a few years to complete at their pace.

As this was going on, Jackie began to teach Eriq about real estate, who, in turn, wanted to create a chain of fitness centers throughout the Southeast region and upper Midwest, called *Buher Fitness*. After careful analysis of other similar chains and speaking with the proper builders, marketers, investors, setting up his corporation and getting the proper licensing, Eriq was finally able to obtain his first gym. Rather than being there, he hired his own employees and purchased some of the most advanced exercise equipment available. He was happy. To finally be in charge of something he now owned never felt so good. He eventually learned how to study reports and analyze data while running mathematical calculations to determine the financial state of the company. As time progressed, he would use that data to make any adjustments needed to enhance and improve the quality of the business. Afterwards, he would discover other areas in which he could invest to create other centers.

It was then that he started listening to Jackie about the law of attraction. He slowly began composing his own dream book and gradually read a few books to get his belief level up so that he could become successful.

It was also at this time that Eriq began to almost worship Jackie. He was just so appreciative of the woman he married, and amazed by her potential and will. And as a sign of his gratitude, he arranged with a floral company for a perpetual delivery of their most elegant flowers every Thursday to Jackie. Eriq chose Thursday since that was the day of the week they first met. Eriq never forgot that day. He would always tell anyone that it was that day when his whole life changed for the better. To him, having Jackie was more important than any professional baseball contract. So in a way, he was kind of glad he had that knee injury.

Though, Eriq was not done. He knew that a woman's birthday, Valentine's Day, Mother's Day, the holiday season and wedding anniversary were five of the most special days of the year to any woman and that they should never ever be forgotten in life. Therefore, he made sure that Jackie received something special on each of those days.

For instance, on Valentine's Day, he would arrange for a hand-picked diamond necklace or bracelet to be delivered to Jackie with roses. While on Mother's Day, she was scheduled to go to a special spa where she was treated royally by the staff followed by dinner for the two of them at a fancy restaurant. Eriq was definitely a thoughtful person and loved Jackie so much. The way he planned each event was so unique and calculated. It was ingenious!

Throughout this time, he hardly took credit for any of Jackie's fortunes. He just was appreciative to have her in his life and always told anybody that the reason he was a better man was because of her. Just hearing those words made Jackie melt into a sweat along with the thought of wrestling him down to the floor and making passionate love to him. That's how much he touched her. She was his forever and so was he to her. Together, they were inseparable. Jackie would later be labeled, "*Miss Thang*" by Eriq, as a compliment to the woman she now was. In addition to all this, their sex life was spectacular; more so than when they were dating.

When the flowers first came, Jackie was just in a loss for words. This first week they were a beautiful arrangement of fragrant white lilies and deep red roses. She did not know what to say. In response, Eriq would just say to her, "don't say anything." It was his gift to her for being the woman that she was and he thanked her for not listening to him. To have a husband who was that appreciative was all she could ever ask for. It made her feel so valuable. The items she received from him were just a bonus. She had gotten her wish, a true soul mate. All she could thank was the Lord God and Mandi, for showing her the light. This time, she had finally discovered what true love really meant, which confirmed that despite her past, there were plenty of good men in the world. It was all in the perception. It was a happy home she had longed for which she finally found.

But it was clear: The Buher family was rich. Though the hunger for more business and clout was ever present in Jackie's mind. As more and more income poured in, she delved into additional projects such as creating her own fashion and cosmetic lines. For the fashion line, she wanted to engage in designing casual wear for adults as well as children, which she called *JB Wear*. As for the cosmetic line, she wanted to manufacture make up including eye shadows and skin care products. It was a tedious project but she enjoyed every minute of it, and within a couple of years, she was able to launch both product lines, with contracts to have them sold in a few major retail outlets.

While all these events occurred, Jackie started appearing in major magazine and news articles. She was a guest on certain talk shows and was a spokesperson for a number of products. Her face appeared on the cover of *Enter-prize Magazine* and she was selected as one of the top 100 richest African-American female entrepreneurs under the age of 40 in America. She also had a number of joint ventures with famous celebrities and business owners that were in progress. And she came to know a few politicians, whom she developed close bonds with. All this was just magic in the air.

Yet with the family around and the dream home still in progress, Jackie felt there would be no better education than to take the family and travel the world. Since her children were always exposed to the family businesses, they had no time for conventional schooling, which resulted in Jackie setting up a home school program for them. That to her was the best education one could ever give their child. This way, a parent controls and monitors what their child learns, which was always much faster and more valuable than most traditional schools, Jackie reasoned.

However, Preston couldn't travel with the family during the summer months as a result of the court order that was finally administered. According to the judge, Preston was to spend summer months with his mother, Sophia, and return to Eriq from late August to early May. Therefore, Eriq had Preston eight months throughout the year, which would continue until he was 18. Yet Eriq made sure to make it up to him as soon as the summer was over. As for Preston, he resented the whole arrangement of even having to see his real mother. Yet, it was necessary for him, and even Eriq understood that. So, for the next four summers, Jackie and the family travelled all over the world. In America, they saw the Grand Canyon, Yellowstone National Park, Mount Rushmore, the Lincoln Memorial, The Statue of Liberty, and other famous landmarks. They had been to many museums and went to Disneyland a number of times. They also visited Hawaii half a dozen times, which was always so addictive.

They went to the Bahamas, including Atlantis Bahamas, Jamaica, Tahiti and the Virgin Islands. It was always such a treat to go to the islands. There, they discovered so many nationalities and ethnic groups. The waterfalls and slides were an enjoyable experience. In terms of food, they savored the best seafood ever. Jackie and Eriq enjoyed many different tropical drinks as they watched many sunsets. It was like heaven on earth. The family also went snorkeling, viewing all kinds of fish underwater as they swam. The natives to those islands were always humble and friendlier than Jackie had experienced in the United States. The hotels where the family stayed were right on the beach, where the couple could watch the kids play in the sand.

To just experience the look on their faces as they would chase each other, laughing and playing, was something words could never describe. It would just bring tears to Jackie's eyes, seeing them feel so happy and secure, which made her think of Mandi. Jackie just wished she could see it too, and see what value her investment in time did to her. As far as financial security, Jackie had already set up trusts and mutual funds for all her children, thus securing their future. They would never endure the pain, anguish, or hardship she had as a child. To even experience a world like this, coming from a world of physical abuse and neglect, before serving time in prison for violent crimes as a high school drop out with no family to go to, was a concept even she had difficulty grasping. All she knew was that the gift of thought made anything possible. Anything. With the right attitude, the right thinking, and patience, whatever one wants can happen.

In Africa, they went on a safari, meeting all kinds of tribes. They then went to West Africa, visiting Nigeria and Ghana. They were so amazed at the diversity of those countries. For instance, in Nigeria alone, there were over 300 languages and dialects, and the language changed every 50 miles, depending on the location one was in. The country was divided into 30 regions, each of which had its own local government. The size of the country was gigantic compared to how it was depicted in the map. It had as many as 80 million people and was the size of Texas. In visiting these countries, they completely abolished the idea that such people ever came from trees, or lived in huts.

Then, they travelled to South Africa, where they stayed in Johannesburg and observed the modern buildings and the behavior of the people, which was similar to the United States. Most of the city appeared westernized, where very few people wore traditional or native attire as they went about their business. It was really interesting.

They went to Egypt to view the ancient Sphinx and Pyramids. The family rode on camels, which was especially fun for Precious. She loved animals, and most of all horses. When they got there, they began to touch and feel all of what they only saw in their history books. It was beautiful.

In France, they saw the Eiffel Tower and relished all the French food that was around them. Jackie most especially loved the different malls that were in Paris, where she bought designer clothes and fancy jewelry. Eriq knew not to shop with her since it was destined that she would take up the entire day. Next, was Germany, where the family saw the Berlin Wall, and explored famous museums.

In India, they went to the Taj Mahal, which had always been a dream of Jackie's. The onion-shaped roof tops and the entire scenery, was just so breathtaking. Inside the beautiful monument were countless pieces artwork that would leave anyone in awe of the human mind. They then travelled to Hong Kong to savor the special kinds of food the city had to offer. Then finally, they went to Japan.

Their final destination within this span was Australia, where they went to Sydney for two weeks and took in the Sydney Opera House. The structure was so unique and interesting. They also went to the local zoo and observed kangaroos and koala bears. Afterwards, they went to the Great Barrier Reef to do some snorkeling, which was near their hotel. The entire journey was an adventure; an adventure none of them would ever forget. It brought fun, education, awareness and appreciation of what the world had to offer. Just to see how her children felt from each of their experiences, was enough for Jackie.

When she arrived back in the States, their house was near completion. All that remained were the plants and the swimming pools that were currently under construction. As for the business end of things, everything seemed to be going well.

She still had liquid cash coming in. Her cosmetic and clothing lines produced modest results while her investments were yielding bigger returns. It was like nothing skipped a beat.

Calls from different people and businesses that wanted to speak with Jackie came in non-stop, most of which were handled by her secretaries and lawyers. If it were really that important, the callers knew how to reach her directly. As for Eriq, his business was doing fine. He decided to open at three more outlets within the coming years. He also decided to create workout videos for people interested in staying fit. It was a long and arduous project for Eriq, and was met with a number of setbacks and disappointments, but he eventually got it done. By the following year, his videos became one of the top ten selling fitness programs.

A few months had passed and the house was finally finished. It was nothing short of phenomenal. All the elements of the home that they planned were there. Precious and Prestonwere blown away. The four-car garage contained the family's luxury vehicles, which were: Mercedes E55, Land Rover Discovery, and Eriq's personal favorite: a red Ferrari F430. Boy could it move! He called it *Desire* in reference to the film, *A Streetcar Named Desire*. The Rolls Royce was, of course, a vehicle driven for only special occasions. Yet its interior (as well as the outer style) was enough to make anyone not want to leave the car once it was driven.

The entrance of the home had a marble foyer that was bordered by the beige Italian carpet that was used throughout the house. The circular stairs leading to the second floor was about 20 feet in front of the entrance way. The master bedroom had two walk-in closets, which contained 32 pairs of Jackie's shoes and an array of famous designer clothes she wore, some of which had the price tags still hanging. The children had their own walk-in closets, full of simple play outfits and tennis shoes. By this time, Precious was 9 and the twins, Max and Miles, were 6 years old. Eriq, on the other hand, had also a nice closet of mostly designer suits and alligator shoes. In addition to the seven bedrooms that they wanted, was a room that was strictly used for styling and cutting hair. And right across from that room, was a private library that contained numerous books on growth development and other subjects. This was essential in supporting Jackie's study habit. She understood early on that all leaders are readers, and thus felt it necessary to have a library of her own.

The dining room and living room each had beautiful chandeliers hanging from the ceiling. And at nearly every corner of the house were paintings, masks and statues placed at specific points of interest. There were also fresh plants throughout the house, thus giving a positive, energetic feeling to the home.

Outside of the house was a mini basketball court and a tennis court. There was also an open field to play football or baseball. And at the center of the back of the house was a 20 by 30-foot pool with a message on a platform below the water that read: *Dream Big,* which could be seen looking downward through the ripples of water.

The barn was Precious's pride and joy since she adored horses. However, Jackie planned to hire a professional caretaker for the horses until Precious came of age to raise them herself. The house was definitely going to require gardeners, maids and butlers, and would require at least $11,000 alone in monthly upkeep expenses, separate from the payroll.

The pool would require cleaning every three months, the rose bushes would need hedging, the grass would need cutting, the fruits and vegetables would need picking, the garden required water and maintenance, and the horses had to be tended to and fed. So a lot came with the house. Yet, Jackie was aware of all this and had plenty of investments to support the costs. Though, she had been instructed by her accountants not build a house of such magnitude for a while.

Upon all this success, Jackie decided it was time to do something that would benefit people. She had a lifestyle people could only read about in magazines or fairy tales. But after traveling around the globe and seeing so many people in need, and recognizing the lifestyle in which she came from, she realized how blessed and fortunate she was. She had learned so much. She had seen so much poverty in so many countries that she decided in some way she needed to help others. So, she decided to create a motivational audio program that centered on the law of attraction and the principles of developing a positive mental attitude. She also wrote a short book on the power of belief.

The book was simply a short story of her past that she shared in order to show people that anyone was capable of achieving success. It was an emotional book for her. However, she decided that it was something that just had to be told so as to reach out to people. It wasn't long before her audio set and book received critical acclaim, and she began going on tour to different parts of the country.

12

⤳⤳⤳

Unity

A<small>T AGE</small> 37, J<small>ACKIE WAS TOURING THE COUNTRY</small>, discussing her book and audio sets. She was a talented speaker. She initially was booked in small halls and high school gyms. But, as her fame grew, she began speaking at convention centers. Businesses and organizations from all over offered her as much as $100,000 for just a few hours of her time to speak about goal achievement. The following July, she signed a contract to speak to a large audience in Austin, Texas, at a local university. Since it was summertime, she brought her family on the trip. The event was remarkable. She could feel the electricity in the auditorium as soon as she got on stage. Claps and cheers filled the room. But as soon as she started to speak, there was utter silence.

Jackie was a natural. The clarity of her voice and conviction in her tone were captivating, thus giving people the sense that whatever came out of her mouth was gospel. The introduction and her speech took almost two hours in total.

When the event concluded, noise erupted. Her fans began waving their books around, hoping she would sign them.

What many people didn't know was that she had developed her confidence in speaking through speaker training classes. However, those classes had about the same impact on her as what she had learned from the books she read by author Dale Carnegie. After reading his book, *How to Win Friends and Influence People,* Jackie became eager to read the other books of his that focused on social skills. No other book delivered that type of effect on her. So, when she searched around for other books by him, what she found were:

The Quick and Easy Way to Public Speaking
How to Develop Confidence and Influence People By Public Speaking
Public Speaking and Influencing Men in Business
Tips for Public Speaking Selected from Carnegie's Original 1920 YCA Course Book

All four books were powerful. They offered her nearly the complete recipe for handling any situation or adversity when dealing with people. The books had really propelled her confidence, which made her fearless when talking to people in either big or small groups, and of almost any personality. She had read each book at least twice. After her speech had ended that afternoon, Jackie began signing her fans' copies of her book. Of course, she couldn't sign everyone's book, but nonetheless, she made the effort. She also shook hands with a few guests as they took pictures. As usual, this continued until it was almost evening, but to her, it wasn't a chore. She enjoyed every minute of it. Soon, the crowd began to leave, except for a few people who were still waiting in line, waiting to shake her hand and take pictures.

"Jackie? Is that you? Is that really *really* you?" asked a familiar voice.

Jackie took her time for a moment, and within a split second, knew exactly who it was. "Mandi!" she screamed. "Oh, Mandi!"

She then ran up to Mandi to hug her, clutching her as hard as she could, almost crying. "You don't know how much I've missed you. It has been such a long, long time," she said.

"I know," replied Mandi. "I missed you too. You have no idea how much I've waited for this moment."

"Me too. I was almost about to put myself on a TV program hoping someone might watch my story and find you for me. You know what… can you please stay here for a moment? I just want to finish greeting these people. It won't take long. I promise."

"Certainly. No problem. I'll be right here."

Jackie then rushed over to the line of the people still waiting for her and began greeting them hastily, hoping now they would all just go away. Mandi had brought her husband, Ronnie, and their three children to the event, and all were waiting anxiously to meet Jackie. When all the fans had finally left, Jackie went back over to meet her longtime friend and mentor.

Bt this time, Mandi, who was now 51, appeared a bit older than when she first met Jackie. However, the change was slight. Her face had that glow of a woman who was only 40. The only major change were the few strands of white hair that appeared at different angles of her head whenever she turned. Yet, she was still attractive, always continuing to show those bright teeth of hers that shined whenever she smiled. She was still as full of life and energy as she was in her younger years. She appeared to still be in good shape as well, with only a few pounds added since she last met Jackie. So she still took good care of herself.

As soon as Jackie returned, Mandi spoke. "You know, it had to be a twist of fate that we're even here today, because my son Riley, who goes to school here in Austin, has always been interested in the law of attraction and invited us to come to this seminar. But I had no idea that you used the name 'Jackie,' so I never knew it was really you until we saw you on stage."

"Well that's how the universe works, remember? You taught me that."

"Yeah, that's right. That I did. But let me first of all introduce you to part of my family. This here is my husband, Ronnie."

"Hello," he said.

"*Hello*," responded Jackie's family.

"And over here, is my daughter, Daisy. She just graduated from NYU School of Drama. She's an actress now."

Daisy greeted and shook Jackie's hand as well as those of her family. Like her mom, she grew into a beautiful young lady.

"And finally, these are my two boys, Riley and Lucky."

"Wait," Jackie said. "At work, I remember you telling me you had two girls and just a boy."

"Well at the time, I *had* two girls and a boy. My oldest daughter, Honey, is now married and lives in Dallas with her husband. They have two kids. But about a year after I left being a parole officer, Lucky was born. Somehow he managed to just... *sneak* up on me," she said while nudging Ronnie against the shoulder. "But it was because of that, he got his name. But you know, I wouldn't trade him for anything in the world. He truly has been a true blessing in my life; a Godsend."

"Hi," Lucky said with a smile.

Lucky then greeted Eriq, but when he approached Precious, a strange thing occurred. Their eyes connected simultaneously, locking for a few seconds, which, in some divine way, felt like an eternity. The two of them just froze, as if the world was standing still.

"Hi," he eventually greeted to her.

"*Hi*" Precious replied, smiling.

"My name's Lucky."

"I'm... Precious."

"And that, you are," he said. "That, you are."

Precious giggled. "*Thanks*," she said.

"You're welcome."

Precious then started blushing, looking downward without knowing what else to say. She was shy. Lucky, on the other hand, just observed her every gesture. He was always smooth with his words. Both Mandi's and Jackie's families, who all saw this, just chuckled in the background. But afterwards, Jackie then shifted back to Mandi to continue on with their conversation.

"So what are you doing now?" Jackie asked.

"Well, me and my husband have to drive late tonight to meet a guy in the morning about investing, and we can't miss it because we tried so hard to meet him to... "

"Cancel it!" Jackie demanded. "Spend some time with us, just for the evening."

Mandi looked at her in amazement. "But I can't. I have to... "

"Of course you can," Jackie then took a deep breath before continuing. "Listen, Mandi. Do you see all this here? Do you see my husband? Do you see my kids? Do you see me? All this that I have right now is because of you. Now of course, I could have decided not to listen to you. I know that. But it was you, a total stranger to me at the time, who came into my life, opened the door, and showed me the way to all this happiness that I feel every day, which no one else on this planet could have ever done for me. And I know that this may seem wrong, but I owe everything that I have because of you. That is why for the life of me, I can't let you just leave me right away... especially after being apart from you for... 14 years. If there's nothing else, let me just owe you a bit of my time. Whatever this cancelation may cost you, I can double it or triple it, no problem. I will pay for any inconveniences. Besides, I don't believe energy brought the both of us here just to say 'hello.' It had to be for a reason. So I'm asking you, actually I'm begging you... spend the evening with us. Please."

"Yeah mom. Let's stay," Lucky interrupted, suddenly.

"Yeah c'mon, stay," invited Eriq, as well.

Soon after, Max and Miles followed suit along with Precious. Then suddenly, a chant of "stay, stay, stay" began from all the kids. From then on, it was apparent: Mandi wasn't going anywhere. Jackie then hugged her and began gathering all her belongings, speaking to the staff of the auditorium, before directing everyone to their limousine that was parked outside. Jackie already had reservations at an upscale restaurant called *La Gore*. It was one of the fanciest restaurants in town. Celebrities would frequent the place whenever they passed through the city.

When they got there, the host found Jackie's reservation but implied that they could not accommodate the extra guests, since they weren't on the reservation list. Jackie then demanded to speak with the manager, who appeared within moments. Jackie approached him privately, explaining the matter, and with a slip of a $100 bill, everyone was accomodated. They were directed to a large table, where each family sat across from the other. Jackie was directly across from Mandi, Eriq was across from Ronnie, while Precious was across from Lucky. Max and Miles sat across from Riley and Daisy.

Shortly, everyone began ordering. Eriq especially wanted Champagne, which was later delivered. The wait was a bit long, but it gave plenty of time for Jackie and Mandi to catch up with each other.

"So, what happened to you after you suddenly left me?" asked Jackie.

"Well, you know the system. The people didn't like what I was doing and demanded that I leave or else, in their own words: 'make it difficult for me and my family.' So after I left, I must admit, things appeared a bit rough. I had no job and just found out that I was pregnant with Lucky. So life did throw me a curve ball a bit. But as usual, everything eventually worked itself out. A couple months after the incident, my husband happened to get a big contract here in Texas, where we ended up moving to. It was then I found my calling to set up an organization to help troubled youths locally and hopefully, nationally. It started out slow but I continue to push on, doing the best I can… for about 10 years now. It sort of has been challenging, because I need the funding to continue reaching out to these kids. That's why I needed to meet with that investor. Oh, I just hope to God he didn't decide to… "

"Say no more," demanded Jackie, sipping her drink slowly. "Just tell me how much and I'll write the check."

Mandi thought really hard, then, as if by magic, a bigger idea struck into mind.

"Oh… I got it! You know what?" she asked. "How about you and I become partners? I mean after all, you're sort of doing what I'm doing, but at a larger scale. But with the two of us, we can really reach out to those that need our help. We can develop schools and programs. It would be our organization, called… oh, I don't know. Let's call it the… M… J… Academy, and its main mission will be to empower individuals like I did with you. It would be phenomenal!"

Jackie suddenly got excited. She was speechless. The only gesture she could muster was to smile and shake Mandi's hand.

"It's a deal" she said. "You see, now don't you think missing that trip to see that man was the best thing in the world?"

Mandi glared at her with a smile. "Both that and meeting you again," she said.

Soon after, everyone received their meals. Dinner was delicious. Yet Mandi and Jackie kept on talking. "I hope all of you have room for dessert," said Jackie. "I hear they have the best desserts in town."

After the meals, the families continued talking. Before long, Jackie then brought up a subject that had been bothering her since she and Mandi last met, 14 years ago.

"Mandi, if you can remember back when we last met, I asked you why you really devoted your time and energy with me and other clients about the law of attraction. After all, it wasn't your job. I just feel there's something more that you just weren't telling me. I mean, what did I really do to deserve all this?"

Mandi then looked around, before staring at Ronnie. "What do you think, dear? Should I tell'em now?"

"Yeah. I think you should tell them," he said. "I'm sure they'd all want to hear all about it."

"What do you think kids?" she then asked. They all agreed with their father except for Lucky, who was too busy talking to Precious, who Mandi had to eventually alert to pay attention.

"Yeah, tell us," implied Max and Miles. "Tell us." Those two were always the nosiest bunch at times like this. Yet, everyone was in support.

"All right," Mandi answered. "I'll do my best, but listen very closely because it's sort of a long story. *So…* here goes."

She grabbed a glass of water, drank it slowly, straightened her shoulders, glanced at the ceiling, took a deep breath and began. All eyes were now on her.

※◇※

At the age of 12, Mandi was diagnosed with cancer. The news was devastating. Though, no one could explain the reason. Never had such a disease ever been known to either side of her family. Her father could trace all the way back to his great grandparents and there was no known member who ever had the disease. The same applied with her mother. And based on the fact that none of their other 10 children were ever that sick, everything seemed so strange. It was so strange to the point that the family went in search of different medical opinions. All confirmed that deadly word.

During the time of the gruesome murder of Emmett Till, segregation and racism dominated Mississippi, which was where Mandi's family lived. But because of the status that blacks had at that time and specifically in that region, Mandi could not get the proper treatment for her disease. And as time wore on, Mandi's health continued to deteriorate. Now, Mandi's family came from modest means. So even if they had access to the best health care possible, her family could not afford it. Though they received a clear message that regardless of their financial status, because they were black, they would not given the consideration to be recipients of more advanced care.

Her mother, Thelma, had served as a maid for a wealthy white family in the country side, where she rode a bus to and from work every day for 20 years, putting in over eight hours a day. Mandi's father, Charlie, was a blacksmith. Some of her siblings were married, while others performed odd jobs to help support the family. Out of all of Mandi's siblings, only three went to college.

A few months had passed and Mandi continued to lay in her bed, gravely ill. She had difficulty standing or sitting without feeling miserable pain in her lower back and legs. She also had massive headaches. She continued to moan and cry, complaining of her condition. Her mouth was always dry and she often felt too weak to do much of anything.

By the following week, she was sent back to the clinic, where the doctor later reported that she had only 4-6 months to live. There was nothing else that could be done, according to him, and he advised the family to start making funeral arrangements. From his "analysis," there just wasn't any hope left and death was inevitable.

Mandi's mother, in turn, was distraught and stormed out with Mandi and Charlie. The entire family was overwhelmed and devastated. Here stood the child whom they all loved and adored, and now there was nothing they could do to save her.

With limited education and not knowing what else to do, her parents turned to prayer on numerous occasions, attending church with Mandi and the children, hoping by some divine intervention, Mandi wouldn't leave them just yet. But still, her condition worsened. Then one day, about a couple of weeks after the family received the diagnosis, Thelma was at work in the kitchen of the estate she worked in, when suddenly she dropped a tray she was bringing out to serve the owner's guests for dinner. The crash was so loud that Francine, her employer, heard the noise and quickly rushed into the kitchen to find out what was the matter. Normally, if any noise occurred, Francine would have allowed Thelma to handle it, but since Thelma had never dropped any guests' meals before, this had to be serious, she thought. She could just feel it.

When Francine got there, she saw Thelma crouching in the corner of the kitchen, sobbing. Francine immediately went over to her. "Thelma dear, what's the matter?" she asked.

Thelma was crying, with her hands in her face, shaking her head. "It's my daughter, Mandi. My baby. She's gonna *die!*"

"What do you mean she's going to die?"

"She has cancer and the doctor says she has only four months to live. I don't know what else to do. I mean I've tried everything, and I can't stand the thought of losing my baby. And she's only 12. She hasn't even experienced life yet and now I'm going to lose her. Oh Lord, why? Why? Why are you doing this to me, God? What have I done? I tried everything… "

"Listen, calm down," Francine ordered.

However, Thelma kept wailing so loud that others began coming into the kitchen to see what was wrong. Francine, however, wrapped her arms around Thelma, indicating to all that there was nothing to see and that they should continue on with their meal. Then, without knowing what else to do, Francine spoke firmly to Thelma, and instantly caught her attention.

"Now look, Thelma. Either you get yourself together right this minute and listen to what I have to say, *or* be ready to put a whole bunch of flowers on your daughter's grave, which will happen a lot quicker than what the doctors predict. I assure you. You understand? So you decide right now!"

At that instant, Thelma was quiet.

So Francine continued. "Now listen, you have served us well all these years and have always been good to us. I appreciate that. You never called off nor were ever once late for work. All the others came and went but you have been here, and I'm grateful for that. I really consider you as part of the family. So I'm going to help you. Now, what I'm going to share with you is something that is so powerful, so proven, that it can help your daughter get through this cancer, provided you do everything I say. Understand?"

Thelma nodded. "Yes'em," she answered.

"As always, just call me Francine. Now I have guests right now. But what I want you to do is clean this floor up. Pick up all the food off the floor. Wash the dishes. Then after you're done, I want you to leave early so you can rest and relax, trusting that everything will be fine. You will still work but only half of the day for the next few weeks. The other half will involve me teaching you and your daughter about this energetic power, step by step, that can help heal your daughter and save her life. Okay?"

Thelma gladly accepted. With her working half the time now, she understood her pay would not be as much to support her family, yet realized that if what Francine was going to share was really that valuable, it had to be worth more than a million paychecks.

Within the next couple of weeks, Thelma pushed Mandi in a wheelchair over to Francine's home. As soon as she arrived, Francine could see Mandi sitting helpless in her chair. Francine then started off by reading special paragraphs from certain success books on how to live healthy. Later on, she gradually began teaching her about the law of attraction and how thoughts are things, which send out vibrations from the mind that attract responses from the universe. Granted, Francine did not have to do any of this, but someone had done the same for her many years ago.

Francine was born into a poor Irish family, known as the *Sullivans,* who immigrated to the United States from Ireland during the Prohibition era when she was only 8. She was the oldest child in her family. The family eventually settled in New York before moving to southern Virginia, where the floor of their new home was filled with dirt covered with hay. Her father, a former bootlegger, later became an alcoholic. Her mother was a seamstress.

Life was rough for Francine growing up. She would walk a couple miles down the road nearly every day, carrying firewood for cooking and pales of water for the house while her drunken father stayed at home, doing nothing, which in turn led her mother to become bitter, venting her anger out at anyone who stood in her way. As the sole provider, the obligations were often too overwhelming, and the only way she knew how to deal with it was to take it out on everyone else.

Their home had only one bedroom, which had an uneven floor where Francine, along with her four siblings, slept. The clothes that they wore were always dirty and torn since each child only owned three pieces. There was hardly any food to eat, which caused a lot of sickness in the home.

In fact, it was the result of starvation that led to the death of her youngest brother, Samuel, who was only 2 years old. It was a horrible experience for Francine, and she shed tears whenever she looked back on it. Yet, those conditions compelled her to dream of a better life for herself. She would close her eyes and enter a world of luxury, security and pleasure. That was what she wanted. She was just so tired of being poor.

She was eventually taught the secret by a wealthy woman named Mary Jo Allen, who was the mother to a little girl whom Francine instinctively saved from an oncoming vehicle on her way to a store. In return for her bravery, Mary Jo taught Francine about the law of attraction. And as fate would have it, Francine used the technique to eventually marry the son of a wealthy landowner at the age of 19. His name was John Williamson. Though, to avoid his father, who was against the marriage, due to Francine's poor economic status, John decided they would move away to Mississippi and start a family, which was how Francine met Thelma and hired her as a maid.

Before she moved to Mississippi, however, Mary Jo told Francine to use the knowledge and someday share it with someone else, which would in turn bless her and all of her family. And thus, it was Thelma and Mandi, along with a few others whom Francine shared the secret with.

As Mandi began learning more and more about the law of attraction, she began developing the ability to feel good and pretend as if she was already healed. She was to smile all the time and discuss nothing negative at all. During this time, she began eating organic fruits and vegetables, as suggested by Francine. If she could, she was to find something to laugh about, which would always raise her spirits. This was very important, because according to Francine, laughter created an alkaline state in the body from which no disease could exist, since the alkaline levels produced from laughter enabled the body to be able to produce healthier cells. In order for it to be a habit, Francine suggested that Mandi laugh for at least 20 minutes a day about anything, and magic would appear. Along with this, Mandi also collected pictures of her goals and dreams so that she could always focus on them, and feel good about them.

As time wore on, Mandi's health began to improve. She had already passed the four-month mark that the doctor predicted she would not live beyond. She was suddenly active and her aches had little if any affect on her ability to move or walk. She soon began running again. Later that year, Mandi's parents took her back to the same doctor for blood tests. The results were to come back within a few days as usual, but for some reason the family never received it.

They went back the following week, but the doctors were unwilling to release the report. Then, out of frustration, Thelma stormed into the office demanding the results. The doctor, who was totally frightened, answered with a stutter, explaining that he along with other doctors were still trying to find out what had happened, because there was no way of figuring out how Mandi was suddenly cured. The cancer was completely gone!

Not knowing what to do, Thelma screamed with tears of joy, and suddenly rushed toward the doctor, kissing him on the cheek. Though the doctor remained motionless, hoping in some strange way that Thelma wasn't a witch. It was a case he had never seen before.

"Alleluia! Alleluia! Thank you Jesus!" she yelled.

When she told the family the good news, everyone was excited, praising God. It was then that Thelma baked a big cake for Francine and took Mandi to see her. When they arrived at her house, Mandi presented the cake over to her. They all celebrated. Francine was so delighted.

"Thank you. Thank you," Francine smiled. "Honestly, you didn't have to do this. But still thank you anyway. I do truly appreciate this gift, but the only way you can truly thank me is by sharing this knowledge with someone else. And in time, you will be rewarded immensely. Just pay it forward."

It was those last two sentences that stayed with Mandi forever. She would soon go on to high school and earn a scholarship to attend college in Detroit, where she eventually met her husband, Ronnie. From there, she continued on to become a school counselor before finally becoming a parole officer.

Someone who was white, who didn't know her, was willing to spend their time to save her life, because that same thing was done to her. It was a pivotal point in Mandi's life. She just could never forget that. Thelma also kept reminding Mandi to share the secret with someone else, which Mandi promised she would do. She was fascinated with the whole subject and promised to educate someone else.

"I know you will," her mother once said with trust. "I know you will. Besides, you'd make a great teacher. I can see it in you already. You have what it takes."

But, by the time Mandi turned 31, her mother had passed. Francine died four years later at the age of 80. Yet, Mandi was determined to fulfill her mother's dream, knowing some way, somehow, she would be staying high in the sky feeling mighty proud of her daughter.

As her story ended, a waitress poured Mandi another glass of water, which she drank slowly. Everyone in Jackie's family, including Jackie, sat still in amazement with jaws dropped. There was utter silence at the table. Even Precious was impressed.

"*That* was why I decided to share that with you," Mandi concluded, blotting her eyes with a tissue. It was an emotional moment for her.

"And you've succeeded," replied Jackie, almost in tears, herself. "You *have*. Thank you."

Mandi soon reached in her purse and pulled out a picture, showing it to Jackie. It was a photo of Mandi and Francine together in the backyard of Francine's villa a year before she passed. It was a beautiful image of the two of them together. Jackie stared at it closely, wiping her eyes, before passing it along to Eriq and the rest of her family.

"Is it possible you could make me a copy?" she asked Mandi. "I know I never knew Francine, but... I just would like to look at it from time to time as memory of how it all began. I mean… your story was fascinating."

"It sure was," added Eriq.

Mandi smiled. "Thank you both," she said. "That's no problem. Of course I'll send it to you."

At this point, it was almost midnight, and the restaurant was closing in less than an hour. Both families wanted to stay longer, but it became obvious that this was going to be the beginning of a fruitful and long-lasting relationship between them. Every member of each family enjoyed each other's company, especially Lucky and Precious. There was a certain energy that made every person feel as if they were with long-lost relatives of some sort.

Shortly after, they exchanged hugs and left the restaurant. Jackie's limousine took them all back to the parking lot where Mandi's car was parked. As soon as the limo got there, Mandi's family hopped out.

"Well Mandi, you take care. I have your number now and you have mine. What we'll do is get together this Saturday and discuss details, okay?"

"Sounds like a plan. I'm looking forward to it. Good night."

Soon after, Lucky got out of the car, but before finally leaving, he turned to Precious. "So how 'bout I write you some time?" he asked her.

"All right," she replied. "I have your address now. So I'll write you, too."

"Okay, well bye. Take care of yourself." He then stepped one foot back into the limo and shifted a bit inside, waving to Jackie and Eriq.

"Bye, Mr. and Mrs. Buher. Thanks for the food. It was delicious," he said.

The couple waved back, greeting him. And, at that instant, he rushed over to the car where his family waited. He was such a gentleman, which excited both Eriq and Jackie that had them trying real hard not to say a word. Minutes later, both vehicles sped away, honking their horns at each other before going in opposite directions.

As soon as the limo left the lot, Max and Miles began teasing their big sister. "*Precious has a boyfriend! Precious has a boyfriend!*" they sang.

Precious then took off one of her shoes, pretending to attack them. "Shut up. He's not my boyfriend. He's just… a new friend."

"Exactly… a new boyfriend," Miles replied sarcastically. "I saw you talking to him. You almost didn't finish your food, because you were that so much in *looo-ve*."

"And you took down his number," Max began. "And he took down *yours*. And look, you're still blushing."

"Shut *up*!" demanded Precious. "*God*, I hate you guys. You guys are *so* retarded! You all get on my nerves and make me sick."

However the twins persisted. "*Precious and Lucky sittin' in a tree, K-I-S-S-I-N-G. First comes love, then comes a baby, then comes a baby in a baby carriage!*"

Precious then threw her shoe at them before punching each of them in the waist.

"Okay settle down now kids. Enough is enough," said Eriq. "Okay, Precious is right. She doesn't have a boyfriend," he smirked. Jackie then laughed too.

"Daddy. Mommy. Stop! He's *not* my boyfriend!" she yelled.

"Of course not, honey. We know. It's cool," Jackie replied.

However, she couldn't help laughing and neither could Eriq. Precious could do nothing but dump her face in her hands, shaking her head. She was so embarrassed. The ride back to their hotel was 20 miles, and throughout that time Precious couldn't help but think about Lucky. She just stood sat in the corner, staring out the window, oblivious to what was around her.

She was only 12 and Lucky was 13. She hadn't that much experience with boys. She always occupied her time by either practicing martial arts, playing with her dogs, Oscar and Roger, or just riding horses. Therefore, the concept of boys never entered her mind. But for some reason, when she met Lucky, everything changed. There was some energy about him that she just could not ignore nor explain.

It was like sitting on sticky bubble gum. Initially, one could pretend as if the attachment doesn't mean anything. But after a while, that attachment makes it impossible to focus on anything else. And if nothing is ever done about it, that stick then becomes annoying. That was the way Precious felt. No matter how hard she tried, she couldn't stop thinking about Lucky, who was just a guy she met. But the more she tried to focus on other things, the more she thought of him. In essence, she liked what she saw and just couldn't explain why.

Meanwhile, Lucky had a bit more experience than Precious, regarding the opposite sex. He would watch funny romance comedies about women and relationships. In fact, most of the smooth lines he could deliver came from watching those movies, listening to music, or listening in on conversations between his siblings and their significant others. He also liked love songs and smooth jazz. He never had sex but had a little curiosity about girls. To him, there was some kind of mystery about them that he just wanted to unveil. And as far as Precious was concerned, he wanted to know more about her. What interested him the most was her smile, her shyness and just the way she carried herself. It was all so exciting to him. He couldn't wait to see her again. The same rang true for Precious. She just couldn't wait to see *him* again. They had such a fun time together.

Jackie, on the other hand, found the whole scenario to be quite cute and fascinating, and was eager to see what would become of it. She was proud of Precious and decided not to interfere with her new friendship unless necessary. To Jackie, maybe, just maybe, Precious was starting to experience what it was like to fall in love; just as her mother fell for her father. Though only time would tell the outcome.

In addition to all the dramatic events that took place that night, Jackie seized the moment to finally tell Eriq some surprising news in front of everyone in the limo. She turned to him and grabbed his right arm, holding it gently in her hands.

"Honey," she said.

"Yes?" he replied.

Jackie looked him in his eyes, smiling. "Congratulations! You did it again. I'm pregnant!"

Everyone just roared. They were now expecting child number four.

13

≫≍≪

More Adventures

URING HER PREGNANCY, JACKIE CONTINUED HER speaking engagements. While this was going on, she and Mandi drew up a concise plan as to the nature of their mission. Since Jackie was often consumed with other ventures, the partnership didn't take effect immediately. Although, Jackie decided that she would soon make time to focus on this since she considered this to be very important. As her condition began to show, Jackie started to relax more and slow her activities down a bit, which according to Eriq, was a healthy choice.

As fate would have it, Jackie was going to deliver another set of twins. She didn't know this until her third month of pregnancy. The most interesting part however, was that this time, she was going to have a boy and a girl. Everyone was so excited. When Mandi heard the news she commended her, but urged her to take time off after the delivery. Soon, they would work out the business details regarding their new venture since they both agreed that they were going to do it, period. It would be called *The MJ Academy*.

Jackie took Mandi's advice about resting, and in the early spring of the following year, gave birth to Miley and Eriq Jr. This time, she swore up and down that there would be no more children, at least from her, in the family. This was it. There was now plenty of company to keep everyone in the household occupied. No one now could ever complain of loneliness and Precious now had a sister.

Preston, now 21, began an apprenticeship at father's fitness chain. Like his dad, he also liked staying fit. He handled the business reporting as best as he could, working with the oversight of the accountants and investors, of course. In his youth, he wasn't as involved as his father would have liked him to be. However, Eriq understood early on to be patient and allow his son to mature into the man he was supposed to be, and when he was ready, he could run the business. *Buher Fitness* was doing extremely well as far as growth was concerned. By now it had grown to nearly 15 outlets.

Eriq and Ronnie began communicating frequently as well and eventually partnered with one another. Ronnie would be contracted under Eriq to construct and remodel commercial outlets for a few future fitness centers, so as to see how their partnership faired. Eriq enjoyed his relationship with his other contractors, although to Eriq, it would be special if Ronnie worked for him, since after all, their wives were working with each other. For Eriq, he felt a strong personal connection with Ronnie that he didn't have with any of his other partners. All that mattered was for them to sit down together and arrange some kind of deal. And in time, that was exactly what they did.

After a full six weeks since her delivery, Jackie finally regained her strength, thanks to the help of her personal trainer and best friend, Eriq. She now was ready to take on Mandi's business proposal. Jackie, who was a very active woman, cleared her schedule for the next two weeks, devoting all her time to her partnership with Mandi. Mandi, who still lived in Texas, was going to meet Jackie at her magnificent villa in Georgia.

When Mandi got there, she was blown away by the size of the home. She couldn't believe all the butlers and maids who came immediately to assist her. She was standing on a marble floor that was shaped in a big square. Wow, she thought. It was just... luxurious! The nanny who was taking care of Jackie's two newborns was right upstairs, carrying one of them.

Jackie and Mandi eventually travelled to the guesthouse to have their meeting.

"Wow, I can't believe you have all this. Everywhere and everyone looks so *nice*."

"Thank you. I try to keep it that way."

Shortly afterwards, a couple of lawyers, a marketing professional and three investors arrived at the house, as planned. Jackie showed them to the guesthouse. It was where all the signing of contracts and legal documents would take place. When they arrived, they were greeted with trays of fruits, vegetables, salads, crackers, bread rolls, and a 1982 vintage bottle of wine to celebrate with. Even though it was just basic signing of paperwork, Jackie always wanted to give her guests a taste of her hospitality. Also, she saw it as a celebration of a long and successful relationship with the woman who was indirectly responsible for it all. Within 30 minutes, all the papers were signed and *The MJ Academy* was born.

During the first months, Jackie and Mandi conducted a lot of research on how to establish their business. For this to work, they had to find other people who were knowledgeable about the law of attraction and could teach it. Those people had to be excellent communicators and also have good people skills. Jackie and Mandi's main objective was to set up a school or learning center where youths as well as adults could be educated on the subject. Each student would also be supplied with books, a training audio and other supplementary materials. Since no known organization had ever done anything like this before, Mandi and Jackie knew had to be extra careful and take their time in developing the project. The both agreed: Rushing into it would be foolish.

Another concern was determining how they were going to design their centers. What facilities were necessary for the business? Of course, there were going to be computers, desks, chairs, large screen video monitors–and beautiful artwork throughout the facility that would bring about a sense of warmth.

So, for the next few months, the partners began making phone calls and travelling to different places, trying to find the right personnel to run their program. It was a long and arduous exercise, but eventually, one by one, people emerged from different places, vowing to uphold their mission.

Mandi and Jackie eventually found the right designers for their center as well. The designers were well experienced and shared in the vision of what they wanted the facility to convey. After careful study, it was decided that their first center would be located in Atlanta.

They figured that because Atlanta was such a big booming town, known for its infrastructure and corporate headquarters, it would be the perfect place to start. Plus, there were a lot of local smaller businesses, which gave the impression that there were a lot of like-minded people interested in opportunity. In addition, even though the cost to attend the center would be a bit substantial, there appeared to be a number of opportunistic people willing to pay for the class.

They knew that in starting any business, there's never a guarantee that the venture will succeed. However, they strongly believed theirs would succeed. Though it may start off slow, they weren't going to give up on their mission, especially since to them, it had to be done.

The format of the program would go like this: The center, which Jackie termed as a "camp," would be composed of two separate groups. There was the youth group, for ages 13-17, and the adult group, for ages 18 and over. No matter the ages within those parameters, the material would be taught the same for that particular group, from the moment a student entered the program. Classes for the youth group would be held from 8 a.m. to 3 p.m., while the adults would attend from 8 a.m. to 4 p.m..

Since Mandi had already put some thought into this idea before reuniting with Jackie, she already had worked out how the sessions would be conducted. During her research phase, Mandi attended some business classes and studied the nature of how schools are run and the key elements needed to sustain them. So, for the most part, Mandi was in charge there. Jackie was of course allowed to contribute any ideas of her own, however her primary responsibility was to run the finance side, from providing the funding to overseeing the accounting, which was no problem for her since she already had the proper staff for that. To create some type of leverage and less risk in their business, Mandi and Jackie allowed for 25% of the entire stock to be owned by multiple partners, while they controlled the rest.

After several months, their first training center was finally established. It was called *MJ Academy*. Surrounding the building was a beautiful yard with a few trees. The interior was designed with lots of color and a variety of beautiful artwork lining the hallways. On the left side of the facility was the computer lab. The adult classroom was across the hall, filled with modern desks and chairs and a large video screen. The next room was set up for the younger group, with circular tables instead of desks and a large colorful carpet. A couple of rooms remained closed since they were empty. They were intended to become classrooms when the demand required it. At the back end of the hall were a couple of rooms where the teachers had their offices. The facility was clean and ready for business.

The tuition for attending the Academy was set at $6,000 for adults and $4,000 for the youths. Since the Academy didn't engage in conventional schooling, the youth session only ran from early June to late August. However, the amount of detail that would be taught during that time frame justified the costs, Jackie and Mandi reasoned. During the session, each child would be invited to take a trip a specific destination in the U.S., where they would stay for a few days. For instance, they may visit the estate of one of the Jackie's close friends, who would share more about how the law of attraction changed his or her life. This was something that Mandi and Jackie believed was vital. It was a way of breaking away from traditional education, by offering the students the chance to expand their minds through personal experience. All costs associated with the trip were included in the tuition. The entire curriculum was set up to reinforce the concept that no thought is too great or too small for the universe to create.

As for the adults, their sessions would last approximately five months, from either February through June or September through January. And similarly, the adults would go on a trip, in their case to an exotic location most had never been to before. The goal was for every student to dream bigger dreams and believe that it is possible to achieve anything. For the youth, this message was especially pivotal since they would be the future. Overall, *MJ Academy* wanted to instill the message that whatever direction a student chose to go in life, first you can become a great man or woman through this education.

During the summer, the youth curriculum would require each student to read five preselected books and discuss them in the class. The instructor would also design and give lectures on the human mind (at a level the students could understand, of course) and slowly incorporate the law of attraction into those lectures. Later into the session, each student would be required to write an essay on any miracles they experienced in their life through using the law of attraction, which was to be read aloud to the class.

Reading aloud was an important part of the curriculum as it would help the students to conquer any fear of stage fright or public speaking, Mandi and Jackie thought. If needed, students would be offered counseling, based on using energy healing to boost confidence. Students would be taught the importance of encouraging their peers, and encouraged to do so, so that no student would feel threatened in this environment. The program would conclude with a family picnic, and each student would then be given a set of books to take with them to read, followed by a certificate of completion.

This same system would apply to the adults. However, the training would be a little more advanced and move at a quicker pace. And since it was a five-month program, adults would be required to read eight books and give their analyses. There would be a few tests or quizzes administered at both levels to ascertain each student's knowledge of the material. Since *MJ Academy* wasn't a conventional school, a student's grade wouldn't affect them in any way. All it indicated was their level of understanding, and in some cases, the teacher's level of teaching, Mandi and Jackie figured. All scores would reviewed by an administrator.

The partners agreed that the Academy would not be concerned with those students who did not want to fully engage in the training, since that only reflected a waste of money on their part. Only those who were very serious about learning the material would excel. Though in reality, Jackie and Mandi were a bit skeptical about the number of students who would put forth the effort needed.

The first year, they experienced lukewarm results. As with any first year, not everything went perfectly. How could it? So they continued making adjustments. After awhile, positive news about the program began spreading, giving the partners the momentum to open more centers in other parts of the country. Years went by and soon the partners had centers in Los Angeles, Houston, Phoenix, Detroit, New York, Washington, D.C., Philadelphia, Memphis and Miami. It was like there was a massive explosion and the demand for the training kept growing.

Certain people who had became successful as a result of the course became spokespeople for the program and some even donated money to the Academy just to express their most sincere gratitude. This was just one of many responses Mandi and Jackie received. It was exhilarating to witness the effect the program was having on the lives of so many students. Just the happiness, tears and hugs the partners received from their former students showed a level of gratitude that no words could ever describe. It was a remarkable journey with amazing results.

Jackie and Mandi decided to give a substantial amount of their profits to charity, helping to support other causes they believed in. It got to the point where they took back only 15% of the Academy's profit after expenses, and the rest went to other causes. They were also able to reduce the tuition and offer scholarships, which made it possible for more people to have access to the program, because in truth, they wanted it available to everybody.

As for Eriq's business with Ronnie, things got off to a slow start. It took Ronnie a while to find the right staff since the work was at a faster pace than he was used to. But after a couple years, things really improved and work was being done efficiently. It wasn't long before Eriq's outlets through Ronnie's hand were opening up in different regions of the country. Eriq also continued to do well with his workout videos and real estate projects. Therefore, he could easily stand alone as a multimillionaire, but would never forget the wife who helped get him there. So for the Buher family, everything appeared nothing short of magical. And the same now went for the Harris family. Daisy, who was now engaged, got a starring role in a major play and couldn't wait for the opening.

❦

As the years passed, Lucky and Precious remained in close contact with one another. They wrote letters, texted and emailed; saw each other at family outings; and even travelled together with their families to Jamaica as a getaway vacation. It was amazing just how much the two of them had in common. They both loved animals, but in different ways. Precious had an immense love for large animals, especially horses. To her, horses were the most beautiful creatures on earth. She was also conscience of the threat of extinction, and at age 16, decided to become a zoologist and began learning about different animals. She took the opportunity to explore the globe, including East Africa to study the many different species native to that region.

Lucky was also a lover of animals but was more interested in animal photography. His dream was to someday work as a photographer for a magazine such as *National Geographic*. If not that, maybe he could have his own show filming different adventures with wild animals, he thought. He knew that whatever he was going to pursue as a career had to include animals of some sort. To him, they were almost like humans. From both of their interests, it was clear that they each enjoyed traveling. To Lucky and Precious, travelling was education, and education was fun. There were just so many great things to explore and their love of animals fueled that interest. Yet as the fun flew by, so did the time. Lucky and Precious were no longer children. At this point, Lucky was now 19 and Precious was 18.

One day they visited the Houston Zoo together, touring around the path, observing the different creatures. As usual, Lucky was taking photographs of the animals in their habitats. It was a perfect spring day, though Precious was a bit uneasy. She had finally decided to bring up a subject that had been troubling her for quite a while.

"Lucky," she said.

"Yes," he answered.

"How long have we've known each other now?"

Lucky glanced at her awkwardly. "Uh, about… five or six years now," he said. "Why?"

"Well, we've known each other this long. We hang out together sometimes. We call each other on the phone. We've even written to each other in the past. We've once travelled together… and I keep asking myself, 'What are we really doing?'"

"What are you talkin' about?" Lucky asked, focusing his lens.

"Will you just look at me for a second? I'm trying to say something."

Lucky turned towards her. Precious then took a moment to gather her thoughts. "Okay, thank you. I'm trying to make a point here."

"Which is?"

"All I want to know is that since we've spent all this time through the years, you've never told me… whether… we're a pair or not. I mean I haven't seen you with any other girls, but… I don't want to be the stupid one assuming things. So I want to ask you now, are we an item or not… or are we just… *wasting* time here?"

"What do you mean, wasting time? I mean I thought we're just… you know… friends."

"So we're *not* an item, is what you're saying? Right? We're just… *friends.*"

"I didn't say that either. I just… "

"So what are you saying? Either we are or we're not. I mean it's like being pregnant. Either you are or you're not. There's no inbetween. I mean, this isn't the seventh or eighth grade. We're both adults and we should both know what the other feels. You've never told me anything… "

"Anything about what?"

"About how you feel about me."

"Well I feel you're a wonderful woman. I mean you're fine. You're fun to be around. You have a nice body. You got good character; nice attitude. You have a nice smile. You love nature. I love nature. Your family's cool. You're respectful. You're smart. I mean... "

"Lucky! Let's cut the bullshit for a fucking minute! Shall we?"

Precious then stopped for a moment, suddenly realizing she was getting too loud. She then relaxed and continued on. "Okay, sorry about that. But to make a long story short, let me just make it in plain English for you to understand. Are you my boyfriend or not?"

"Wh... What? Am I... I guess so. I mean... "

"There's no guessing, Lucky. I may be 18, but I have a life. And I am not going stay around and waste my time over you to make up your mind when I... "

"But wait," Lucky interrupted. "You never told me about how you feel about me. So I just thought... maybe... you weren't that too interested. And I didn't bother asking. So... I guess we were just... you know... hangin' out. I mean I don't know."

"Well, we don't have to just hang out any longer. If you want to know how I feel, I'll tell you."

"I'm listening."

Precious then organized her thoughts for a few seconds, preparing for what would bring either a pleasant or unpleasant surprise from Lucky. She was a little timid at first. Yet she eventually said it anyway with confidence, just as her mother would have. "I've loved you since the moment I first laid eyes on you. And it's a feeling that won't go away. I enjoy every moment we're together, when we talk on the phone or write each other letters. And I would make you the happiest man in the world as your girl."

As outspoken as Precious was, even *she* couldn't believe what she had just said, and for a moment, felt as if she had just literally spilt her guts on the pavement she was standing on. Yet she still awaited Lucky's response while looking down. There was nothing but awkward silence for nearly a minute, and she suddenly became disappointed and walked away, embarrassed.

"Wait," Lucky said. "Come here."

Feeling dejected already, Precious just ignored him and continued on.

"I love you too," he claimed. Precious then turned around, suddenly looking at him with a sign of hope. "And it would be an honor to be your man," he added with a smile.

Precious smiled as well but tried controlling herself since Lucky was a jokester at times. "Are you serious?" she asked.

"Look at me," Lucky said. "Does it look like I'm playing? I've never been more serious in my life. Honestly, I *do* love you." Lucky then took a couple steps forward, looked directly at her and stretched out his arms. "Com'ere," he said. "Come *here*."

Upon hearing that, Precious put both hands over her mouth in excitement and ran towards him jumping in mid air. At that instant, Lucky instinctively caught her, almost dropping his camera, as she kissed him all over his face and neck, while wrapping her legs around him. "I promise to make you the happiest man in the world," she said.

Lucky looked at her with a smile. "I know," he replied back. "Say, let's get out of here and go back to my place. I'm done snapping."

"Sure," she replied with joy, while still in the air.

Moments later, they were at the Harris home. It was a gorgeous mansion, which Precious and her family had visited a number of times. When they got there, no one was home, except for a couple maids, which Lucky anticipated. He held Precious's hand, directing her upstairs to his room.

As soon as they got there, Lucky shut the door, grabbed an audio remote and turned on a Boyz II Men CD. He then dropped the remote, approached Precious without hesitation and made passionate love to her. It was an exciting moment neither of them would dare forget... ever! As for Precious, she was not only in love, but in heaven. And whenever someone's in heaven, he or she doesn't want to go anyplace else. Yet in the back of her mind, Precious was wondering: *What in the world took Lucky so long?*

While still in the room lying down, she turned towards him and asked him that same question. In response, Lucky shrugged his shoulders before reaching under the bed to pull out his own dream book he had been writing in, which he opened in front of Precious. He turned a few pages before pointing to one of his goals, which had stars right next to it.

Precious tried to look at it carefully, but before doing so, she saw the preceding pages which were full of photographs that Lucky had taken of her on different occasions. She then glanced at Lucky, smiling before eventually going back to the line he was pointing to.

In it read: *I wish for Precious to belong to me and only me... FOREVER.*

And that was no joke. He meant it. As soon as Precious read that, tears instantly fell down her face. It was the sweetest line she had ever read in her life. Lucky then made a comment.

"Sorry it took this long, but honestly... I just... I guess... I didn't know how... how to come at you straight and tell you. I figured... you might tell me first. I guess it was just... pride."

Precious shrugged, saying, "Men... "

Then, she slowly kissed her boyfriend on the cheek, looking him straight in the eye. "It's okay now, because none of that matters anymore. But I must say this, you forgot one important thing," she said.

"What's that?" he asked.

"You never put down how many kids you plan on having with this woman."

"Well, okay. I want uh… maybe three or four."

"That's it? I want six! I mean, I'd like six… very much. That's only… if we get married, of course. Is that a problem?"

"Is that a problem? Sweetheart… it's only a problem if I was a woman. But as a *man*, I don't mind dishin' it to ya *every* night. *Believe* that! I'm more than capable for the job."

Precious laughed. That was another thing she loved about Lucky. He was always so funny. At one time, she encouraged him to do standup comedy. "I just can't wait to tell my mom," said Precious, elated. "She'll be thrilled. All this while she kept wondering what was going on, and all I could tell her was… *nothing*! Now I can tell her *everything*… except… *this* of course. She doesn't have to know that one. But I'll tell her everything else."

Lucky turned away momentarily, knowing that Precious would eventually tell her everything since that was the type of woman she was. She had a habit at times of letting words just slip out without knowing it. And this was no exception. Yet he loved her anyway.

"Just one thing," reminded Lucky.

"What's that?"

"Now I know that this is in all women, so don't feel bad. But… just try not to be too complicated, okay?"

Precious looked at him, rubbing his cheek. "Baby, your wish is *my* command," she said with joy, before kissing him softly.

Lucky smiled before contemplating something else he wanted to say. "You know, Precious, my parents must have known what they were doing when they named me *Lucky*."

"Why's that?"

"Because I always feel that way whenever I'm with you."

Just then, Precious was speechless, consumed with emotion.

"Now you know if you keep this up, we'll have a baby in no time," she mustered. "I'm warning you." They both laughed.

"But it's the truth," he admitted.

There was a slight pause between the two of them as both their eyes gazed at each other. "Well, in that case... I'll make sure you continue to live up to your name... *always*," replied Precious while kissing him repeatedly.

Lucky smiled again. "Thanks," he said. "That's all I needed to know."

They looked into each other's eyes before Precious suddenly remembered something. "Oh, I just remembered. I've been reading this book called *The Five Love Languages* by Gary Chapman. It's really good. It teaches how anyone can make any relationship last forever through thick and thin."

Lucky's eyes opened. "Really?" he asked.

Precious nodded happily. "Yup! I noticed for a while how my mom would carry it with her wherever she went. So I went and got it to know what was in it. Now I know. So don't worry, sweetie. We'll be fine. I'll give it to you to read some time. But for now... where were we?"

Lucky just looked at her tenderly and said, "Baby, now you know I can show you better than I can tell you. *Com'ere.*"

From there, it didn't require a genius to figure out what happened again. And since neither of Lucky's parents were going to be home for days, the two of them had plenty of time together.

14

⫸⫷

Full Circle

Nine years had passed since Mandi and Jackie's reunion at the auditorium in Texas. And during that span, so much had happened. They went on many adventures together, travelling the world, spreading their mission. This was especially a dream come true for Mandi, since travelling throughout the world had been one of the chief goals she wrote down while battling cancer.

Eriq and Ronnie had also developed a great relationship. Ronnie got contracts solely from Eriq to build his fitness centers, which now numbered over 50 outlets, nationwide. By this time, *The MJ Academy* had grown into a billion-dollar empire, with over 20 camps nationwide, having educated nearly 100,000 people of all ages, since opening. What was most impressive, was that its students, both past and present, came from almost every background imaginable, both in ethnicity and lifestyle. This didn't even include the audio training sets, which had been selling in the millions. The response was overwhelming. Thousands of letters came continuously from past students and their relatives, who hailed the program and gave testimonies of different miracles that had occurred in their lives. And from all of this came a heavier demand for the program.

There was soon a waiting list procedure instituted. Depending on where the camp was located, some waiting lists took longer than others to fulfill. Mandi and Jackie soon realized that they needed to expand, again. They were elated with their success. In essence, they were changing the world. Their eventual goal was to take this program global one day, to where they would have a few camps on each continent.

From the wealth of the company, money was never a problem again for either partner. Whatever Mandi or Jackie wanted was attainable. There was almost nothing they couldn't afford. They were respected wherever they went, meeting prominent figureheads and celebrities throughout the world. They were now in the category of the 1/2 of 1% of the population that held that kind of wealth.

So, when Lucky and Precious decided to get married, there was no doubt that their wedding would be nothing short of spectacular. It was going to be the talk of the town, to say the least. Celebrities and business moguls would be there. It was going to be held in beautiful Fort Lauderdale. The church ceremony would be followed by a reception at a five-star hotel, where the guests would partake in the most exquisite dinner with live music and lavish festivities.

Afterwards, close friends and family would spend the rest of the evening on *The MJ Academy's* yacht. Mandi and Jackie purchased this 192-foot yacht to occasionally take their students on excursions. Mandi and Jackie were especially excited about using it for the wedding celebration. Who would have guessed that such turn of events would ever lead to this moment?

What started with Max and Miles teasing Precious about a "boyfriend" had turned into a reality. Even the twins couldn't believe it. To them, they were just poking fun at their sister. But conversely, it was almost as if they were psychic all along. And as a way to tease them back, Precious would now tell the twins, "See what you guys did. It's all your fault. Next time you boys should be more careful about what you joke about. It just may come true."

However, the twins had developed a good relationship with Lucky over the years, and felt that he would make a great husband for their sister. In all, they were happy that Precious was so happy.

As soon as the wedding day was over, the newlyweds planned to spend their honeymoon in Cancun for 10 days. Neither one had ever been there, so they both chose it as an opportunity for a new adventure. They heard so many great things about it and couldn't wait to go. Lucky, in particular, couldn't wait to rent jet skis to tour the waters.

Yet, the entire wedding was going to require a good six months of proper planning. Everything just had to be perfect. There had to be perfect flowers, perfect dresses, perfect lighting, and so on. The cake had to be magnificent, displayed a high table, and next to it would be an ice sculpture of a horse, to commemorate the couple's love of animals.

When the moment finally arrived, it was like heaven on earth. First of all, there was plenty of sunshine, which gave a great start to the day. The guests arrived first, awaiting the bride and groom. When Precious finally arrived, she was dazzling. Around her neck she wore a beautiful diamond necklace that sparkled from every angle. Her white silk dress was breath-taking, with a train so long it had to be carried by her bridesmaids every time she moved. She wore an elegant diamond bracelet and her platinum engagement ring, that held a four-carat diamond, was moved to her right hand this day. She was beautiful. As soon as Jackie saw her, tears rolled down her cheeks. How the time had passed. All that was running through Jackie's mind at that moment was the memory of holding her baby daughter in her arms in the labor room. Now, Precious was all grown up and about to enter into a new family. She was 21.

Lucky looked both astute and handsome. He wore a designer tuxedo with shiny dark shoes. The scene was far too emotional for Mandi to even bear, and she began crying. Lucky was all grown up. He would be the last of the Harris family to get married, while Precious was the first in her family. Max and Miles were 19, while Miley and Eriq Jr. were only 8.

Max was an interesting teenager. Like his father, he was very athletic, playing many different sports throughout high school. By the end of his senior year, he was ranked within the top 10 high school tailbacks in the nation, with a record of completing 40 yards within 4.37 seconds. He was nicknamed *"Mr. Lightening."* Defenders would only see a blur of him whenever he had the ball. He had an excellent cut back, was aggressive on the field, could block, and was a great punt returner, once scoring a 91-yard touchdown run, which was every coach's dream. Whenever Jackie came to any of his games, she would always shout from the stands: "That's my boy!"

Max was offered several scholarships, but eventually chose to attend LSU. If he stayed healthy and played with the talent he had in high school, professional football was definitely in his future. There was just no doubt about it. He was that good. And he couldn't wait to play. However, he would have to play as a back-up tailback behind the school's senior starter before he could finally start during his sophomore year.

When the church ceremony finally ended, it was off to the beautiful hotel hall. Precious was now Mrs. Harris. A sign on the back of the limousine read: *"Mr. and Mrs. Harris: Together and Forever At Last."*

During the celebration, the guests passed around the microphone and gave their own detailed stories about the couple. There was a band, lots of dancing and lots of delicious yet elegant food. There was lobster, crab, caviar, steak, a variety of salads and a beautiful display of fruit. The desserts were to die for. Before the cake-cutting tradition, Lucky and Precious had a guest share a short prayer for the couple. Afterwards, Precious cut the cake, then slammed it into Lucky's mouth. The scene was hilarious. Lucky did the same, and they each ended up with faces covered in icing. The cake was then cut for the guests. It too, was delicious.

Later, there was, of course, the tossing of the flowers by the bride, which were caught by one of the bridesmaids, while Miles caught Lucky's wedding band. Miles then took a quick glance at the girl who caught the flowers, who was looking straight at him, waving. Miles waved back. The girl was attractive and about the same age as him. Then, out of nowhere, Miles took it upon himself to talk to her. (He, too, was very smooth with the ladies, thanks to his dad.)

"Congratulations, you caught the flowers," he said to her, extending his hand. "My name's Miles."

The young lady gently shook his hand, staring at him closely. "Destiny," she replied.

"Oh, *Destiny*," he remarked. "Well in that case, I better follow you where ever you go, since after all… you seem to *know* my future."

She laughed. "So you got jokes, huh?"

"*Well…* I've been known to have that effect on women from time to time."

"Is *that* right?"

"Yes ma'am… and a whole lot more."

"Then enlighten me, Casanova. I'm listening," she smiled.

From there, the conversation went on. Destiny was actually the younger sister of one of Precious's closest friends, named Makayla. So with that knowledge alone, Miles had no problem getting to know her a little better. Destiny also happened to be a freshman in college with aspirations of one day becoming a journalist. And as for her, she didn't mind Miles's company. It was always a pleasure to know a man whose family had connections.

As they talked, the conversation grew interesting and Miles decided to invite her on the yacht, although she wasn't on the list of those invited to go on board. However, she had no problem accepting. From the conversation they were having, the two of them already seemed to share a connection that was deep and genuine.

Miles didn't really want to take on college. He decided to pursue real estate like his parents. He had always been fascinated with property and felt he had a good mouth piece to close any sale, and was unaffected by anyone who said "no" to him. He was that tenacious. He acquired that same spirit from his mother and from reading books on success principles.

The book *Rich Dad, Poor Dad*, by real estate guru Robert Kiyosaki, was Miles's greatest inspiration, and he had already read it three times. Basically, the book was a classic insight into the different principles that the rich teach their children about money that the poor and middle class do not.

As the party was winding down, the newlyweds received well wishes from many of the guests and then each of them took the microphone to thank everyone for coming and suggested that they take as much food with them as possible.

On the yacht, the celebration continued. Miles eventually took Destiny to some small back room of the yacht where they started kissing. Miles then looked at her. "I don't really do this at all, you know."

"Neither do I," replied Destiny. They both smiled.

"You know Destiny… I really don't know what it is, but… something just tells me that we seem to connect real well. And I just want to say… that… I like you a lot."

"So do I. I… I feel the same way."

Miles then grabbed her hand pulling it closer to him. "So what happens from here?" he asked.

"What do you mean?"

"I mean we have only but a few hours left on this boat. I mean soon everyone will be on their merry way and be gone but… I… I mean I… "

"You don't want to see me go," she completed. "It's nothing to be ashamed of. You can say it. *Gosh!* I don't know why you men have such a hard time telling a woman how you really feel. And you guys always say that *we're* complicated."

Miles just looked down trying hard not to answer.

"I don't want to see you go either," she added. "As long as we communicate and talk to each other often, we're not too far away. I'll give you my number and we'll just go from there. Let's just take it slow and see where this all leads us, because to tell you the truth, I'm definitely loving what I'm feeling right now… *boyfriend*."

Miles smiled. "Come here," he told her.

Destiny did and the two of them kissed to where it began to get physical. Destiny was never the type to submit to a man she just met. However the emotion inside her would not allow her act any differently. She wanted him and he wanted her. And later on, to put it mildly, both tried their best not to make too much noise as the platform around them shook rapidly. They were each happy. Very happy.

"Don't you just love weddings?" Miles asked.

Destiny nodded. "Who knows, this may just be a preview of ours."

"Maybe."

"I hope though this won't make you not to talk to me anymore."

Miles looked at her carefully. "Now why would I ever do something like that? I believe it was the law of attraction that brought us here. So I would be a fool not to honor this great miracle."

"Law of attraction? What's that?" she asked.

"Haven't you ever seen the movie, *The Secret*?"

"Uh... no."

"Well don't worry. I'll teach you about it some day. That's if... you let me."

Destiny smiled.

As it turned out, Miles and Destiny would continue on as a couple and later marry in the summer after her senior year in college. A year later came their first child, a baby boy named David, followed by two more boys and a girl. Together, they were a happy family.

Miles would eventually excel as a real estate investor, while Destiny became a freelance journalist. She would soon own a local newspaper called, *Sincerity Press*, which was known for its factual reporting, using only credible sources, in contrast to all the major newspapers that usually lied or mislead all their readers, she thought. Destiny's paper would also offer solutions to certain problems, which led her to discuss the law of attraction, thanks to the help of her husband, Miles, and reading the book *Ask and It Is Given* by Jerry and Esther Hicks. The paper also started covering health-related topics, such as new natural health discoveries and organic remedies to different ailments.

In the end, Jackie would leave behind a fruitful legacy. As for Max, he ended up becoming a professional football player. Eriq Jr. would eventually become a renowned chef, owning a string of restaurants called *Erix*, while Miley took over her mother's businesses, adding a yoga club and a number of health food stores to the portfolio. All three siblings would eventually marry, which gave Jackie a total of 27 grandchildren, including those from Preston.

Jackie always considered Preston her own son, even if it wasn't through blood. As far as she was concerned, it was his action that fateful day of breaking away from her on their walk that lead her to the fortunes she had now. But above all, Jackie never stopped telling Preston that she loved him. And Preston loved her for that. They would always remain in close. As for Eriq Jr., he named his first son Eriq also, which of course meant Eriq III. Hopefully, he too, would take on the family restaurants, just like his daddy.

Yet of all the family success stories, the one that stood out the most was that of Lucky and Precious. A few years after their wedding, Lucky got his dream of hosting his own reality show called *Lucky Adventures*. He would tour different parts of the world, engaging with wild animals, while giving a short history lesson on their behavior. The theme was somewhat similar to other shows, however the show still did pretty well and aired for several seasons. From its revenue, came the funding of the zoo that Lucky and Precious, along with several investors, established in Kenya. Precious became the zoo's animal curator.

It was an expensive project to set up, but not nearly as costly as it would have been if it were in the United States. It took a lot of work, along with the challenges and setbacks. In all, it took much longer to establish than the couple predicted. But still, they enjoyed every minute of it, feeling they were doing the Lord's work. Animals were their passion; their joy. Not far from the zoo was an beautiful home that the couple had built together from the ground up. It was large for the area, with an outside swimming pool, maids, a private chef and a guest house. There were palm trees throughout the property. It was paradise!

Many people back in the states assumed the couple was crazy moving off to a foreign land to live. But in their minds, nothing gave them more peace and joy than living among animals. And the local villagers welcomed the couple wholeheartedly, as if they were their own family. The hospitality was so remarkable that it felt as if they were finally home. Also, they weren't harassed by the various taxes, laws or government agencies that Americans dealt with on a daily basis. The couple was more or less free to establish their own businesses at will, without agency involvement, and to savor the profits.

There also was a prevalent culture whereby the younger generations respect their elders, and contribute work to the household, which indicated a level of structure and discipline in the home. Such values were far less common in the United States, and the couple eventually decided that Kenya was where they would live permanently and raise their family. From Lucky and Precious, came six children as predicted: three boys and three girls. The boys' names were Marcellus, Isaiah and Caleb; the girls were Queen, Mandi and Blessing.

Precious chose "Queen" as a reminder of her mother, Jackie Queen Buher. As far as Precious was concerned, her mother was a true heroine and nothing in the world could ever change that. And, it wasn't particularly because of all Jackie exposed Precious to that drew her to that conclusion. But Precious eventually heard of her mother's full life story.

At first, Precious had trouble believing her mother's story because the woman she knew, as long as Precious could remember, never reflected a woman who came from such circumstances. The mother she knew was always happy, courteous, compassionate, giving and humble. When she heard certain parts of her mother's story, Precious cried, wondering how her mother was able to survive through all that turmoil in order to change. In response, her mother just said that it was through the divine power of the Heavenly Father that it all was possible, by sending His agent, Mandi, to intervene in her life, leading her to the light away from darkness, which she chose to follow, that made all the difference in the world.

This was why she admired, loved and adored her mother so much. To Precious, her mother was so brave. If there was anything Precious's grandmother, Brenda, did right, it was giving her the middle name Queen; because Jackie *was* truly the Queen in her daughter's heart. After listening to her mother's story, Precious thought that maybe a movie could be made of it!

Soon, Lucky and Precious adopted the language, Swahili, and later set up a small school and orphanage center. They also began handing out training CDs on the positive development to local villagers, to help them in their personal lives. The materials, of course, were produced by none other than *The MJ Academy*. They still continued to go back to America to visit their families, usually during the summer months or for winter holidays. And they were good at keeping in touch when they were back in Kenya.

Jackie was just happy that *they* were so happy. That was all she could ask for. And as for Precious, she was happy for that as well.

Though, Precious would soon have more to be happy about. As a result of all the praise and attention the training CDs were getting from the local Kenyans, Mandi and Jackie would eventually get their wish. They would now establish their first ever training center in a foreign land, Kenya. And because they were fluent in Swahili, guess who would run the center? Lucky and Precious, of course.

As time progressed, people from neighboring countries would soon show an interest in the material, and the business continued to expand—thus changing the world forever.

Ahhh… the magical flow of *energy!*

15

⋙⋘

Flashback: Lessons Learned

As Lucky and Precious's wedding celebration continued on at the yacht, Jackie decided to look for Mandi. Eventually, one of the guests pointed her out. From afar, Jackie could see Mandi standing alone near the back of the yacht, staring at the blue ocean, which now stretched as far as eyes could see. Jackie took a few more minutes, watching her closely, before finally deciding to join her. With all the excitement, everyone seemed to be having a good time, except for Mandi, so Jackie thought. Therefore, she wanted to make sure everything was fine.

As Jackie approached Mandi, she continued to gaze into the air, unaware that anyone was there, which puzzled Jackie.

"Are you okay?" Jackie wondered.

Mandi turned to her and smiled. "I've never felt better," she said.

"Do you need me to get you anything? 'Cause I can… "

"No, no, no." Mandi pleaded. "I don't want anything. I just want to enjoy this moment; experience the waves, the cool breeze, and all the colorful things we take for granted. We are always too busy saving the planet, but we never take time to appreciate all nature has given us already."

Jackie, a bit moved by the statement, saw Mandi's point. It was an exercise that even Jackie, herself, rarely engaged in. So at that moment, she decided to stay with her friend and share in the moment.

"Well, why don't we have a seat right here then?" Jackie invited.

A few feet away was a bench that was perfectly suitable for the two of them. Mandi agreed. As they sat, they both remained silent, until Jackie couldn't help but come up with a topic.

"Thanks for giving me the book, *Outwitting the Devil* by Napoleon Hill. I really enjoyed it and will make it a must for all my kids to read. I put it at the top of the list as my favorite book of all time. No man should exist without it. And it's funny, because in a way I sort of feel like I outwitted the devil already."

"You have and… you're welcome."

Another moment of silence came. "Well, we have definitely come full circle," Jackie uttered.

"We have," replied Mandi. "It's a proven fact, what goes around, *comes* around."

"Yeah, and you know it's funny. I first met you when I was 23 years old. Now here we are… 23 years later."

"I know. Isn't that strange? What a coincidence."

"Yeah. What a coincidence."

A pause arose before Jackie brought up another subject. "You know, Mandi, I just look back at my life and all that has transpired and sometimes, I wonder… I just wonder… that from all the probabilities… what if… just what if, I was assigned to a different PO, where would I be now? Would I be dead or back in jail… or strung out on heroin? Or what if I was released a few months later to where they had just let you go? Or… "

"Shhhh… shhh… shh. Listen," Mandi whispered. "None of that even matters now. Remember, the law of attraction is always working with the right matching elements to bring that which you want, to light, which from my energy, was what I wanted. It was my dream to reach out and change a person's life, and the universe brought me you. If it wasn't for you dropping your diary, which led me to read it, it wouldn't have propelled me to spend my time to have concern in teaching you, because it's not every ex-con that I shared this information with. Or maybe the universe figured you were the perfect candidate that would listen and be coachable compared to the others whom I had difficulty reaching. So through its divine power, it brought you to me. So do not worry. Despite all probabilities, the law of attraction has the set formula in place that will make things happen in your life 100% of the time, or else it wouldn't be a 'law.'

"This was why I didn't give you any way of reaching me from the letter I wrote you from years back. I figured that with the books, you already had all the tools needed to manifest any desire you wanted, and if we were ever going to meet again, we would. By not communicating with me, that gave you a chance to grow and create results on your own without needing me all the time. I just figured contacting me all the time would have done you less justice than help you. I wanted you to taste life a little, and referring back to those books would have helped you get through any dilemma or challenge. Trust me, it was a painful thing for me to do, but I figured it had to be done so you could grow, and with time, we would meet again… if it was meant to be."

Jackie smiled, appearing a bit stunned by Mandi's words. She had instituted an attitude of "tough love" for Jackie. And Jackie never knew this was all part of Mandi's plan. After thinking about it, it took Jackie a few minutes to compose her own thoughts, before finally speaking again.

"You know also, Mandi, I was thinking about my mother, and… "

"Shhhh. You shouldn't… "

"No. It's all right. Just please hear me out first."

Mandi listened.

"I was thinking about my mom and all the things that she did to me, and I figured this: Whether right or wrong, she only did what she could from what she knew from prior experiences that surrounded her as a child, and I know deep down, she wouldn't have wanted me to go through what I went through had she been raised in the light. No right mother would. And I'm sure that deep down, she wished she could kill herself than have me experience what I did. But in some magical way, I was brought out of the darkness… through prison, and into the light now, which is why I believe that if my mom's around now, she's looking down, feeling mighty proud that I could do what she couldn't."

Jackie then looked up in the clouds, saying, "It's okay now, mom. I forgive you. I've…*let go*."

Mandi smiled. "I'm sure she knows now," she said. "I'm sure she knows now." She then glanced at Jackie who was now teary eyed, and began rubbing Jackie's back as a means of consolation. "It's okay, darlin'. It's okay. There's no need for that now. Everything's all right now. Okay? Everything's fine."

Jackie just nodded looking down at her lap. "Hey listen to me. Listen to me," Mandi commanded. "Just look at me for a second." Jackie turned to her hesitantly. "You are an inspiration to so many people. Against all odds, *you*, Jackie Queen Buher, did it," Mandi smiled. "You hear me? You did it! You… *did* it! Okay? You beat everyone and everything that ever tried to beat you… whether it was not knowing your father, your mother dying, not getting your high school diploma, having bad friends, drugs, alcohol, prison, the court system... "

"I know. I know," Jackie replied as she leaned against her friend's shoulder. "It's just that it still hurts sometimes. You know?"

"I know. But at least look at what it has given you. It has given you a life anyone would want... especially those who never went through such experiences."

Jackie then thought for a bit, before looking at Mandi again, and smiled. "You know, you've always known how to make the best out of any situation."

"Well of course sugar. That's the secret, remember? Whenever you bring the positive out of any situation, you'll always attract those positive results."

"Yeah. You're right," Jackie replied. "You're right."

Mandi then took a moment to herself before finally deciding to reveal what she had been harboring inside all along. "You know Jackie, I wanted to say something else as well."

Jackie wiped her tears, and turned to Mandi. "Yes?"

Mandi began. "You know, throughout all that we've been through, I've learned so much. But most especially, I've learned so much about you. You know, we've travelled the world and have done so many amazing things together, but still, that hasn't been what has impressed me the most about you. I've seen and observed you closely since the very first time you arrived in my office. How you've transformed! And from that, you have showed me a life that has been beyond my family's wildest dreams. But you know, from all that, it isn't the expensive cars you have, or the nice homes, or the jets, or your clothes, or the jewelry, or the fancy meals we savor all the time that impresses me about you. I mean, don't get me wrong, that's all nice and dandy, and I wouldn't dare want any of that to ever change. Trust me on that. But... my point is: It isn't what you have or have done that has impressed me the most about you."

Jackie, a bit anxious about where all this was going, asked the simple question: "Then *what* has impressed you the most about me?"

Mandi looked at her squarely in the eyes, and with her soft voice, responded. "It's the person you've become that has impressed me the most about you. For you to be able to devote your life, inspiring others and helping raise people from lowly stages as you once were, through teaching them about the law of attraction along with other things, is what's the most telling about you. Your willingness to give back, impact and change lives, and give others a chance that want it, as you were given, tells me the world about you as a human being. That is a sign of *true* character. And that is why each day I am the happiest woman in the world to have you a part of my family. The Heavenly Father has truly blessed me. I couldn't have asked for a better in-law and friend. I love you so much."

Just then, the two embraced, hugging, as tears began rolled down their cheeks simultaneously. It was the first time Jackie had ever seen Mandi cry.

"Thank you so much," Jackie cried. "I love you too."

"You're welcome," Mandi sniffed. "And you know I don't lie. I meant every word."

"I know."

A pause arose before Mandi spoke again. "You know, it's now that I fully understand the blessings Francine said I'd receive if I ever shared this secret with someone else. She was an angel indeed. She always knew what she was talking about, and never once lied to me. Not even once."

"Oh yeah, I did want to ask you about that," mentioned Jackie.

"What is it?"

"If Mary Jo and Francine were here with us right now, what do you think they'd say?"

"Well first of all, since we still think of them, they *are* still here with us. That's number one. Second of all, I think they're right now impressed and amazed with what we've accomplished and can't believe the extraordinary miracles this secret has done to the lives of so many people throughout the world, whom we've affected. I mean, who would have thought such a chain of events would ever lead to this point in our lives? Sometimes *I* can't even believe it. So I *know* they'd probably have a tough time believing it as well."

Mandi paused again before making one final comment. "Jackie, it's just so amazing what the powerful gift of thought can bring to a person once it's used for good. It creates so much magic and energy and brings upon so many gifts and miracles that can occur anywhere. It is so limitless and I already know that deep down inside, Lucky and Precious will be just fine."

The two then looked at each other, smiling. Suddenly, Mandi began leaning against Jackie's shoulder, which Jackie welcomed wholeheartedly. After a few minutes, Mandi's head then rested on Jackie's lap, which Jackie began rubbing gently with her hands.

They stayed on that bench together, remaining in their own world, staring into the beautiful sunset, forgetting all the excitement that was still behind them. It was a magical moment that lasted the entire evening. Neither woman said a word. It was serenity at last; peace on earth.

THE END

"*Whatever the mind of man can conceive, and bring itself to believe, it can achieve.*"

—*Napoleon Hill*

Jackie's dreams came true. Now, what would YOU like to manifest?

Start now by putting your name on the blank line and listing all the things you want in your life. Remember, no dream is too big or too small for the universe to fulfill. After you're done, look at your list every day for 10 minutes and read it aloud, believing it will come in, and discover the magic that will appear into your life.

I, _____, would like to now manifest the following in my life:

Appreciation!

I FIRST WANT TO GIVE UTMOST THANKS TO ALMIGHTY GOD for making this book even possible. In all fairness, I really want to say that this book was written by Him and not me. The ideas and images that magically appeared in my head before even knowing what to write is a phenomenon in itself that I may never understand nor begin to fully explain. All I can say is: thank you, thank you, thank you! I almost never knew how my story would turn out, but somehow, someway, it all made sense once I touched the keypad. Seriously! That's all it took; like magic! It's the simplest way I know to describe it.

To my girls: Uchechi, Ugochi, and Oluchi. I love you all! Your presence alone helps me create better characters. To my parents: Anthony and Anthonia Iwenofu. Thanks for giving me life and supporting me in this project as best you could.

To Connie Swenson Garofoli for being the editor that you are on the second time around. You truly are talented and gifted which is why and how I know everything happens for a reason. So bless you! Hopefully we can do this again.

To John Smagola, my photographer and friend. You are truly a great miracle in my book! To my cover designer: Nate Myers of Wilhelm Publishing and Design, thanks for everything. As always, you have no problem with me!

Special thanks also to Hope Point Press for becoming my publisher and electing me as president while also sharing in my vision *(Hee hee!)*.

I also want to thank attorney, Stanley Josselson, for your wisdom and legal counsel through this matter. To the social medias: Facebook, Twitter, LinkedIn, and You Tube. Your network helped get the word out there. So thank you for being available.

Thanks also to Donna Chumley and the staff of Tate Publishing for wanting to work with me after reading my manuscript. It is just so exciting to know that out of 4% of all the manuscripts you accept, I was among the ones selected. Believe me, that's how I knew I was on my way.

Also thank you Hay House, Inc and Mollie Harrison of Balboa Press for informing me about the system and your services. It meant a lot. And thank you Deborah Burke for your understanding and support. I hope to visit Maine some day.

Also thanks to Tara Foreman, Nancy Glenn, and Dr. Smarty for your "sweet" customer service. The same goes to Keionna Speight, Melissa Shabdu, Elaine Tryon, Deborah Torres, Dr. Raheja, and Dr. Nickles.

To Kevin Trudeau and the entire Global Information Network family and staff. I couldn't have gained even a fraction of this wisdom if it wasn't for your contributions. I hope I am displaying the positive fruit of your labor in the best way possible. To my uplines, Greg Kramer and Brandon Kramer.

Thank you so much for your support, both past and present. I feel so lucky to have you all, and thanks for your patience.

To Mark Hamilton and the whole Neo Tech/Neothink Society and Twelve Visions Party. You helped bring this book to life by helping me envision a perfect world and society for all! I want to as well thank Unity Center of the Heights Church \for the enormous energy you brought to me every time I attended your church. Just the environment, brings an energy that can only be explained once a person attends. To Reverend Tony Senf, you are the perfect example of unconditional love, free of biasness and/or prejudice. You make it clear to everybody that everyone is family and of course... the perfect child of God! To the Unity members: Kathy Sullivan and the Unity band, Reverend Hank Roth, Walter Davis, Neville Hatchett, David Kramer, Sandy Rozelman, Joe Buehner, Bethany Chos, Dawn Richardson, Michelle Federico, Mary Eason, Bri Tanei Roberts, JoAnne Watson, Crystal Watson, Debra Morano, David and Kelly Henderson, Jacqueline "Jackie" Owen, Kathryn Mierke, Mamie Wiley, Myrya Johnson, Ada Perez-Heart, Rose Leininger, Bill, and Leslie Fortney reiki practitioners: Mary and Doreen, followed by Betsee Bruich, Susan Haberland, and Sandy. To Dr. Tracy Harris, thank you for your wisdom and Book Workshop program. Your knowledge is intense and full of wealth. I absorbed every moment of it. All I ask is that you hang in there. I can smell the scent of success for you already.

You helped inspire me. So don't you ever forget that. To Michelle "Mama Kimba" Posey and Amber Harris, thanks for your contribution as well. To Charissa Murphy, thanks so much for helping bring natural wellness through your health products.

To all the authors, both living and dead. You've all inspired me all the same. I want to first start out with my biggest hero, Napoleon Hill. Any day I pick up any of your books, I'm reminded of who I am and what I'm capable of being, which is still a small fraction of my overall capabilities. So thank you. Trust me, your 20 years of research was not in vain. You inspired me! Next is Og Mandino. As I mentioned earlier, books create ideas and your classic, *The Greatest Salesman in the World*, became the catalyst that compelled me to write this series. So thank you. I'm deeply indebted. I may not have been ever able to write this book the way I did without your "help".

Thank you Jerry and Esther Hicks for your books. I really enjoyed *Ask and It is Given* along with *Money and the Law of Attraction*. They are one of my all time favorites. The way the law of attraction is explained, is done in such a simplistic pattern that can only prove that it has to exist! To Rhonda Byrne, thanks for helping develop the book and movie, *The Secret*. It is a great eye opener to anyone who has never heard about the law of attraction or knows what it means, which is why I used it in the story. You brought awareness to all.

To the rest of the authors, I salute you. So I will begin my list. Wallace Wattles, James Allen, David J. Schwartz, Claude M. Bristol, Norman Vincent Peale, Dale Carnegie, William Danforth, Russell Conwell, Frank Bettger, W. Clement Stone, Robert Kiyosaki, John Gray, Kevin Trudeau, Peter B. Kyne, J. Paul Getty, Zig Ziglar, Francis P. Martin, Don Gossett, Maxwell Maltz, Chinua Echebe, Ngugi Wa Thiong'o, Allan Patton, Jesse Ventura, Jim Marrs, and David Icke.

To the motivational and inspirational teachers and leaders: Michael Beckwith, Les Brown, Wayne Dyer, Gregg Braden, Tony Robbins, Tony George, Sandra Bishop, Lisa Ryan of *Grategy.com*, Laura Vabornik, Marci Shimoff, and Jack Canfield of the wonderful series: *Chicken Soup for the Soul*. I want to let you know that I watched the movie: The Keeper of the Keys. That was truly a powerful part you played in! Everyone should check it out. The entire cast was phenomenal! Also to Don Storms, Chris McGarahan, Dr. Leonard Caldwell, Ted

Morter, Blaine Athorn, Mary Miller, Marshall Sylver, and Fred Van Liew. You all are great inspirations to all of mankind!

To all the past MLMs I've been a part of. They have each taught me a lot about freedom and never ever ever ever ever surrendering on my goals and dreams, no matter what the cost. So I thank you Quixtar, Primerica, Tahitian Noni, ITV Ventures, N2K, Avion Energy, and MonaVie for helping me see that. To my GIN brothers and sisters who helped support and inspire me through my journey starting first and foremost with Athanc "AC" Sarantopoulos, his daughter: Mahi and family, Jason Longwell, Shawn Beckley, Cedric "Handyman" Johnson, Dan Westfall, Sandra Panagari, Javon Panagari, Bruce Akins, Doug Halfacre, Renee Maira, Sherri Tenpenney, Jeff Tolle, Beverly Weaver, Margaret Gittens, Jackie Easley LaMont 'The Mindset Coach' Jones, Marlon Spurgeon, Ndubuisi Apu, William Syner, DeMarco Davis, Allen Clark, Leslie Elia, Derrik Landers, Shaprice Smith, Beverly Leppard, Ashley Taylor, and John White.

To Tupac Shakur, "Biggie", Canibus, AZ, Nas, Cormega, Common, Mos Def, Boyz II Men, Maxwell, Sade, and Jill Scott for your inspiration in helping me see a new perspective to writing the story. To Earl Nightingale for delivering that lovely album called *The Strangest Secret*. It *is* the strangest secret indeed.

To Nnena Nkemere for taking care of me during my early childhood. Many blessings to and your family! To the Nigerian foundation: Nzuka Ndigbo. Thanks for the messages and support. To Nigerian friends and family of Greater Cleveland like Dr. Onuora, Azubike Onuora, Dr. Odafe, Lazarus Oranugo, Malichi Nzekwe, Roland Chukwukere, Chris Adigwe, Uchechukwu and family, Grace Ekuibe and family, Edna Isoro and family of Indiana, Bernadette Erokwu, Sam Nwosu, Dedo Bennet, Dr. Stella Iwuagwu, Gertrude Mkpara and family. Thanks Ifeoma and Nkeiruka for listening to me speak in Canton. To Kenneth Aguolu, Ambassador Ignatius Olisemeka,

Ekwuzie Olisemeka. Also to John and Tony Okro along with Ifeoma Okoro. I love being called "The Godfather".

To my lovely aunt and dear friend, Sister Miriam Azode. I love you dearly and please forgive me for not getting back with you. It has never been anything personal. To my beloved cousins: Onyedika Njoku, Okwudile Uzukwu, Inkiru, Kenechi, Father Ike, and Chino Onwukanjo and familyof England. To my other cousins of my fathers side. I still love you all no matter what. To Dr. Elueze and his son, whom I consider to be my "brother", Uche Elueze.

Also to Robert Amoah, Chuck Okoye, Ike Okoye, Amaka Offodile and family, my new found "brother" Buchi Offodile, Lucky Ugoh, Dr. Mbanefo and family, Paul Abiola, Hakim, Sampson Tedunjaiye, Esther Virich, Kenneth Ekechukwu, Leo and Tina Anozie. To Francis Ezepue for giving me a strong laptop that never disappointed me even once whenever I used it to write all three of my classics and beyond. You are a great computer man full of integrity.

To the entire Iwenofu family, the Chukwu family, the Njoku family, Uzukwu family, Ihejerika family, and Okocha family. To Ejike. I still love you, man. We should still "kick" it some day. To Chimezie and the whole Abuji family and Ogbuehi family in Columbus. Also thanks to my former neighbors, Chekwube Ogwuegbu, Junior Ogwuegbu, and Sola Saba. Much love. Keep doing your thing! To my friend, Kim Lee, you take care of yourself.

To Christina Catavoles in New York. Thank you for everything you've done for me and continue to do. Also "hi", Mrs. Catavoles. I'm grateful to have met you. Continue to take care of yourself. You're worth it!

Thanks especially to my dear friend and counselor, Johane L. Stoutt. I love you. You are so full of wisdom and knowledge and a definite life saver! Thanks so much. Remain blessed wherever you are.

To Ken Doyle for the "game" you gave me and introducing me to 'AC' which established a major breakthrough in my GIN business. To Karen Straughter for all that you did for me prior to that. To Sherryona Buchanan for your help as well. Also, to the storeowner, BD (of West 41st), for "helping me out" every time and Matt Nussbum for your great customer service. Again, you never know who's paying attention.

Life can never be called "life" without one also remembering his childhood. So I want to thank Mike and Mark Wahba and his family as well as John Mullin and his entire family. I never forgot our childhood days. We had some good times. The same goes to John and Matt Rispoli. And Randy as well. Also, to my man Shawn McKinley. It's so good to see you again. I also can never forget the boys' and girls' club of Marist Comprehensive Academy in Uturu, Okigwe in Nigeria. It showed me discipline, mental toughness, and how to use ones instincts, which can never be taught. Either you have it or you don't. But at Marist, you're *forced* to have it. Period!

To Recovery Resources and Murtis H. Taylor for sending me clients to house for homeowners I worked for when I could barely feed myself. To Steve Davis, you are truly a God send. Seeing you reminds me that there are still plenty of wonderful people throughout the planet. Also to LaShan Williams. Thanks for your care and support. To Debra Winston of Harbor Lights for giving me the opportunity of working there along with giving me a second chance. Thank you! I learned a lot, believe me.It also helped me write this story.

To the men's breakfast club of the Unity Church at Westlake. It's so much fun to sit, chat, eat, and hang out with men of like minds. It's so empowering! I learned from all of you. Thank you Ted Brewer for inviting me along with the group, Jim Larsen, Jeff Hutchinson, Jeremy Johnston, Carl Collins, and Tom Spence. You guys are great. Thanks also to Reverend Barbara Smith of Unity of Westlake for the amazing job you continue to do as well as the staff. Thanks also to the music conductor Al Buehner, Greg Skuderin, Lisa Simoneau, Michelle of the Course in Miracles along with Gertrude. etc. Also thanks Tolisa Mize Horning. Your yoga class was really uplifting and inspiring. I felt the benefit!

To Father Bob, Deacon Harding, and the entire staff and members of St. Agnes Our Lady of Fatima Church in Cleveland. To still connect with where I was baptized is always something special.

Thank you Bill and Annette Cardwell for welcoming me to your home. To wonderful staff member, Toni Smith. To Ellen Connally, Francisca, along with Eugene and Nkiru Okafor. Thanks for all the sweet things you've done for me and my family. Also to members: Maxine Jackson, and Julio Taylor as well as the church choir and members of the 10am mass. Continue to keep it rockin'!

To Dr. Drost, Connie, Sherry McGovern and the entire HCG Anywhere staff. Your program helped me lose the weight necessary to look my best for the video on my website: *jackiesmiracle.com.*

So thank you. It was well worth the investment!

Thanks also to the Landmark Forum in developing me to become a better person than I ever thought possible as well as all the wonderful people I met during the process.

And lastly, to all those of you who have read my book. Thank you!!! Thank you!!! Thank you!!! Without you, my message is meaningless. But if there was one thing…or excuse me, two things I could say to sum up my message to you, it is this:

You HAVE the power…and it IS always POSSIBLE!

"Remember, believe and succeed. Doubt, and go without."
—*Kevin Trudeau*

In all, I love you. I wish you all the best. God Bless and build bigger dreams! The world needs it as well as the next generation!

Your miracle awaits!!!

—Emeka Iwenofu

Hope Point Press
Its mission. Its purpose.

Hope Point Press is committed to providing you, the reader, with inspirational tools and material that you can use to create more positive change in your life in whatever path you so desire. I hope that you not only enjoyed the story presented, but are inspired to manifest things in your life as well as helping to inspire others. Be sure to go to my blogs for constant material updates designed to nourish your soul with positive inspiration as you go about developing yourself the way nature intended at *TheMiracleTrilogy.com* or any of the websites accompanying the titles of the books throughout the series. In the words of my dear friend, Reverend Tony Senf of the Unity Church of the Heights:

"May the best of your past be the worst of your future."

Always remember that you have the power, and are more than you can ever know.

God Bless!

Emeka Iwenofu
President

Sources

Allen, James. *As a Man Thinketh*. Jeremy P. Tarcher/Penguin. New York, NY. 1902

Bettger, Frank. *How I Raised Myself from Failure to Success in Selling*. Fireside. New York, NY. 1947

Bristol, Claude M. *The Magic of Believing*. Pocket Books. New York, NY. 1948

Byrne, Rhonda. *The Secret*. Atria Books; New York, NY. Beyond Words Publishing; Hillsboro, OR. 2006

Carnegie, Dale. *How to Develop Confidence and Influence People by Public Speaking*. Pocket Books. New York, NY.1955

Carnegie, Dale. *How to Win Friends and Influence People*. Simon & Schuster. New York, NY. 1936

Carnegie, Dale. *Public Speaking and Influencing Men in Business*. Kessinger Publishing. Whitefish, MT. 2003

Carnegie, Dale. *The Quick and Easy Way to Effective Speaking*. Pocket Books. New York, NY. 1962

Carnegie, Dale. *Tips for Public Speaking Selected from Carnegie's Original 1920 YMCA Course Books*. E & E Publishing. Sausalito, CA. 2007

Chapman, Gary. *The Five Love Languages*. Northfield Publishing. Chicago, IL. 1995.

Conwell, Russell H. *Acres of Diamonds*. Jeremy P. Tarcher/ Penguin. New York, NY. 1915

Danforth, William H. *I Dare You!* BN Publishing. Miami, FL. 2010

Clason, George. *The Richest Man in Babylon*. Penguin Books. New York, NY. 1926

Giblin, Les. *How to Have Confidence and Power in Dealing with People*. Reward Books. New York, NY. 1956

Gossett, Don. *What You Say Is What You Get*. Whitaker House. New Kensington, PA. 1976

Hicks, Jerry and Esther. *Ask and it is Given*. Hay House, Inc. Carlsbad, CA. 2004

Hill, Napoleon. *The Law of Success in Sixteen Lessons*. Tribeca Books. New York, NY. 1928

Hill, Napoleon. *Think and Grow Rich*. Jeremy P. Tarcher/ Penguin. New York, NY. 1937

Kiyosaki, Robert. *Rich Dad, Poor Dad*. Warner Books. New York, NY. 1997

Maltz, Maxwell. *Psycho-cybernetics*. Pocket Books. New York, NY. 1960

Mandino, Og. *The Greatest Salesman in the World*. Bantum Books. New York, NY. 1968.

Martin, Francis P. *Hung by the Tongue*. FPM Publications. Lafayette, LA. 1979.

Peale, Norman Vincent. *The Power of Positive Thinking*. Fireside. New York, NY. 1952

Schwartz, David. J. *The Magic of Thinking Big*. Simon & Schuster. New York, NY. 1959

Wattles, Wallace D. *The Science of Getting Rich*. Jeremy P. Tarcher/Penguin. New York, NY. 1910

Ziglar, Zig. *See You at the Top*. Pelican Publishing Company, Inc. Gretna, LA. 1975

The Global Information Network. *Your Wish is Your Command: How to Manifest Your Desires*. Speaker: Kevin Trudeau. CD Audio Set. 2009

Freedom Writers. MTV Films. Paramount Pictures. Hollywood, CA. 2007

The Secret. Prime Time Productions. Nine Network Australia. Melbourne, Australia. 2006

Zeitgeist: The Movie. GMP Films. Turners Falls, MA. 2007

Rich Dad's Academy Training Session. Embassy Suites Hotel Hall. Beachwood, OH. April 8-10, 2009

http://www.barrypopik.com/index.php/new_york_city/entry/to_know_and_not_to_do_is_not_to_know/

http://en.wikipedia.org/wiki/Emmett_Till

http://www.globalinformationnetwork.com/Members/Member-Training/

http://www.globalinformationnetwork.com/Presentation-Video.html

http://www.orgoneblasters.com/mindcontrol-bartley.htm

Article: *Understanding the Reptilian Mind* by James Bartley

http://www.youtube.com/watch?v=WibmcsEGLKo
Keyword: The Greatest Speech Ever Made

http://www.youtube.com/watch?v=ZawpgQ1LyLE
Keyword: Og Mandino – Life Lesson

http://www.youtube.com/watch?v=BskUce3i4IY
Keyword: Napoleon Hill recalls the Wisdom of Andrew Carnegie

http://www.youtube.com/watch?v=JgUc7eLXsOs
Keyword: The Strangest Secret in the World

http://www.youtube.com/watch?v=ajIRxdeCRZM
Keyword: The Strangest Secret (part 1 of 3)

http://www.youtube.com/watch?v=es7UjzlSRcU
Keyword: The Strangest Secret (part 2 of 3)

http://www.youtube.com/watch?v=AuPdzHd8idk&feature=
related
Keyword: The Strangest Secret (part 3 of 3)

Experience the
Miracle Trilogy
Classic Series

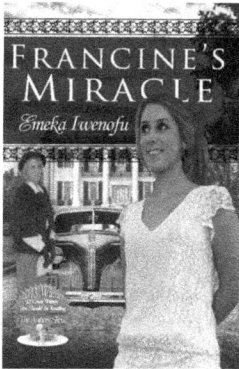

Jackie's mentor

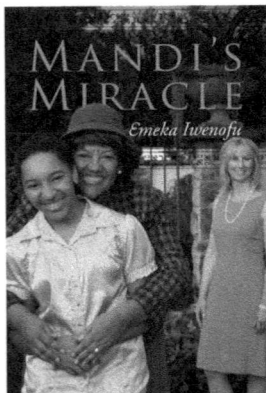

"*When I started reading* Mandi's Miracle, *I thought it was going to be a tragic story about death and grieving. So it was nice when I got to the part where Francine was telling Mandi what to do to get rid of her cancer; it was even more wonderful when it worked. This novel gives hope to readers that no matter what obstacles we encounter, the law of attraction will help us get through it. It is also good to know that whatever disappointments I have, I can just think that maybe it is not meant to be. The story flowed really well, and the incorporation of Francine's lessons was just right. It wasn't like a lecture at all. Emeka Iwenofu wrote this novel in a way that was easy to understand and relate to.*"

—*Lorena Sanqui*
Readers' Favorite

MandisMiracle.com

About the Author

EMEKA IS A YOUNG ASPIRING author WHO ATTAINED A degree in accounting before encountering different detours and challenges in life that led him to pursue his passion for writing while going on a personal mission to help inspire people on how to live abundantly and happily through the techniques he discusses in his series The Miracle Trilogy® which has been adored and admired by fans throughout the world, from which *Jackie's Miracle* has been translated into Japanese with more translations of all three of his books, expected in the near future.

Since publishing *Jackie's Miracle*, Emeka has been busy appearing on multiple radio stations as well as doing weekly blogs on his websites, sharing his mission to the world of positive thought and spirituality and the keys to successful living which he models daily in his life.

He is the owner of Hope Point Press and is the winner of the coveted *2013 Fifty Great Writers You Should Be Reading Award* from The Author Show. He hopes his books continue to inspire people of all walks of life into realizing that they themselves control their destiny and can create a more fulfilling, prosperous, and rewarding life for themselves if they really want to.

www.ingramcontent.com/pod-product-compliance
Lightning Source LLC
Chambersburg PA
CBHW071957040426
42447CB00009B/1373